Normandy 1944

COMBAT

Hitlerjugend Soldier
VERSUS
Canadian Soldier

David Greentree

Illustrated by Johnny Shumate

OSPREY PUBLISHING
Bloomsbury Publishing Plc
PO Box 883, Oxford, OX1 9PL, UK
1385 Broadway, 5th Floor, New York, NY 10018, USA
E-mail: info@ospreypublishing.com
www.ospreypublishing.com

OSPREY is a trademark of Osprey Publishing Ltd

First published in Great Britain in 2018

A catalogue record for this book is available from the British Library.

ISBN: PB 9781472825605; eBook 9781472825612;
ePDF 9781472825629; XML 9781472825636

18 19 20 21 22   10 9 8 7 6 5 4 3 2 1

Maps by bounford.com
Index by Rob Munro
Typeset by PDQ Digital Media Solutions, Bungay, UK
Printed in China through World Print Ltd.

Osprey Publishing supports the Woodland Trust, the UK's leading
woodland conservation charity. Between 2014 and 2018 our donations
are being spent on their Centenary Woods project in the UK.

To find out more about our authors and books visit
www.ospreypublishing.com. Here you will find extracts, author
interviews, details of forthcoming events and the option to sign up for
our newsletter.

Dedication

This book is dedicated to the Canadian military personnel that fought
in Afghanistan as part of Operation *Enduring Freedom*. I would like to
thank Alfred de Boda and Jason Toth for their good humour during my
deployment there in 2006.

Acknowledgements

I would like to thank Martina Caspers at the Bundesarchiv, Eric
Mineault and Anne-Yves Nadro of the Library and Archives Canada,
and Eliza Richardson, archivist at the Laurier Military Archives, for their
help accessing the images used in this book. Lawrence Hong from the
University of Victoria provided access to primary sources pertaining to
the Canadian Scottish Regiment. David Campbell assisted as ever with
the secondary sources.

Comparative ranks

Canadian Army	Heer	Waffen-SS
Field Marshal	*Generalfeldmarschall*	N/A
General	*Generaloberst*	*SS-Oberstgruppenführer*
Lieutenant-General	*General der Infanterie* (etc.)	*SS-Obergruppenführer*
Major-General	*Generalleutnant*	*SS-Gruppenführer*
Brigadier	*Generalmajor*	*SS-Brigadeführer*
n/a	n/a	*SS-Oberführer*
Colonel	*Oberst*	*SS-Standartenführer*
Lieutenant-Colonel	*Oberstleutnant*	*SS-Obersturmbannführer*
Major	*Major*	*SS-Sturmbannführer*
Captain	*Hauptmann*	*SS-Hauptsturmführer*
Lieutenant	*Oberleutnant*	*SS-Obersturmführer*
Second Lieutenant	*Leutnant*	*SS-Untersturmführer*
Regimental Sergeant Major	*Stabsfeldwebel*	*SS-Sturmscharführer*
Battalion Sergeant Major	*Oberfeldwebel*	*SS-Hauptscharführer*
Company Sergeant Major	*Feldwebel*	*SS-Oberscharführer*
Sergeant	*Unterfeldwebel*	*SS-Scharführer*
Corporal	*Obergefreiter*	*SS-Rottenführer*
Lance Corporal	*Gefreiter*	*SS-Sturmmann*
n/a	*Oberschütze*	*SS-Oberschütze*
Private	*Schütze*	*SS-Schütze*

Key to military symbols

CONTENTS

Introduction

By June 1944 the soldiers of 3rd Canadian Infantry Division, the formation of First Canadian Army that would participate in the assault on the Normandy beaches, had spent three years in Britain. All were volunteers and the landings would be their first battle. Battle drill training had taught advanced infantry skills and small-unit tactical exercises had brought them together as a team. General Bernard Montgomery, the commander of all Allied invading ground forces, praised the Canadians' fitness for military service (Milner 2014: 26). Yet the *Official History of the Canadian Army in the Second World War*, written by Colonel C.P. Stacey in the late 1940s, bemoaned their achievements and emphasized the importance of numerical and material advantages, air superiority and better commanders. In the 1990s the Canadian historian John English, seeking to explain the perceived failings of some offensives in the

Unit training for the Canadians above company level started in Britain, where better facilities were available. Route marches were lengthened and large-scale exercises were a regular occurrence. Battle drill served to integrate the different components of the platoon and some officers and NCOs attended Assault Course Schools. Here, recruits attend the Canadian Training School at Worthing in 1943. (Canada. Dept. of National Defence / Library and Archives Canada / PA-177351)

Normandy campaign, blamed operational commanders for not developing doctrine and training capable of defeating the Germans.

Once ashore in Normandy the Canadians' immediate opponents included 12. SS-Panzer-Division *Hitlerjugend*; the division's rank and file were predominantly Hitler Youth volunteers born in 1926, but when the formation was organized in 1943 some recruits were coerced to join. In June 1944 most soldiers were 18 years old and totally unfamiliar with combat. Junior non-commissioned officers (NCOs) were usually only a year older. Senior NCOs and junior officers were in their early twenties and to varying degrees had fought on the front line. With no battlefield experience the division was unlike the majority of other Waffen-SS formations and senior commanders brought in from 1. SS-Panzer-Division *Leibstandarte SS Adolf Hitler* taught them how to be Waffen-SS soldiers; however, the recruits they trained already had military skills that included field exercises and shooting, previously acquired on Hitler Youth weekend camps.

The ethos the Waffen-SS encouraged was to fight with uncompromising aggressiveness and a never-say-die bravado that was heedless of danger but which caused many unnecessary casualties. The Waffen-SS was created from Hitler's personal bodyguard and had expanded from a small company in 1933 to four divisions by 1940. Their purpose was to protect the regime from internal threats and they would serve alongside the German Army (Heer) to win honour and recognition. Political indoctrination taught them they were part of the master race. They were ruthless on the battlefield and not averse to risk during training. By 1943, Waffen-SS Panzer divisions were some of the best-equipped units in the German Armed Forces (Wehrmacht) and their accomplishments were lauded at home. Time and again they were called

The German newspaper *Angriff* (Attack) lauded the Hitler Youth as the source of a new generation of Germans prepared to die for Nazi ideals (Butler 2003: 21–22). SS-Oberführer Fritz Witt, the commander of 12. SS-Panzer-Division *Hitlerjugend*, stressed the importance of physical training, character training and weapons training. He encouraged the relationship between his division and the Hitler Youth by having members of the latter visit to observe training. (Bundesarchiv Bild 146-1987-121-11A Foto: Woscidlo, Wilfried)

MAP KEY

1 6 June: 3rd Canadian Infantry Division lands at Juno Beach. 7th and 9th Canadian Infantry brigades follow up the initial assault and advance either side of the River Mue.

2 0800hrs, 7 June: 1st Battalion, The North Nova Scotia Highlanders (1 NNSH) with 27th Armoured Regiment (The Sherbrooke Fusiliers Regiment) start to advance to Carpiquet airfield in order to establish a blocking position against a German armoured attack. SS-Panzergrenadier-Regiment 25 and II./SS-PzRgt 12 arrive and set up unnoticed by the Canadians.

3 7 June: 1 NNSH captures Buron and Authie from elements of 21. Panzer-Division, but III./SS-PzGrenRgt 25 counter-attacks and Authie is lost by the Canadians. The Germans are able to occupy Buron and despite a temporary withdrawal following a Canadian artillery bombardment and armoured attack, they regain the village because 1 NNSH is severely depleted.

4 8 June: SS-Panzergrenadier-Regiment 26 arrives. I./SS-PzGrenRgt 26 attacks Norrey, defended by 1st Battalion, The Regina Rifle Regiment (1 RRR) and is repulsed. II./SS-PzGrenRgt 26 defeats 1st Battalion, The Royal Winnipeg Rifles (1 RWR) at Putot, but 1st Battalion, The Canadian Scottish Regiment (1 CSR) counter-attacks and recaptures the village.

5 Late evening, 8 June: 15./SS-PzGrenRgt 25 and elements of I./SS-PzRgt 12 advance on the Bayeux road to Bretteville-l'Orgueilleuse. 1 RRR fights throughout the night to defend the village and Cardonville Farm.

6 8 July: Buron and Authie are taken as part of an Allied offensive that targets Caen.

7 9 July: Caen north of the River Orne is captured by the Allies.

8 7–13 August: Operation *Totalize*, an offensive by First Canadian Army to close with US forces enveloping the Germans to the south, fails to break out south of Caen.

9 Early morning, 15 August: 7th Canadian Infantry Brigade, including 1 CSR, is ordered to move on to high ground north of Falaise as part of Operation *Tractable*. At 1000hrs 1 CSR, with a squadron from 6th (Reserve) Armoured Regiment (1st Hussars) in support, is given Hill 168 as an objective.

10 Afternoon, 15 August: 1 CSR advances and captures the hill, despite heavy resistance from III./SS-PzGrenRgt 26 with Tiger tanks in support. Following on, 1 RWR fails to capture Soulagny from I./SS-PzGrenRgt 26.

11 16 August: Elements of 2nd Canadian Infantry Division capture Falaise.

12 16 August: 4th Canadian Armoured Division is held north-east of Falaise, but 1st Polish Armoured Division reaches the River Dives. A link-up with US forces at Argentan will only be secured by moving through Trun.

upon to deal with crises on the Eastern Front. They did not disappoint, using infiltration tactics that sought to break through an enemy line and exploit into the rear area in order to create disorder; the vast expanses in the East offered good opportunities for Waffen-SS tanks to dominate the battlefield. Combined-arms battlegroups (*Kampfgruppen*) were formed, with junior leaders given latitude in how to put together a battle tactically.

Though they had no battlefield experience the Canadians did not think the Waffen-SS, despite their reputation, were superior soldiers. Most Canadian battalions knew that soldiers were being murdered by the Waffen-SS and felt less compunction about not accepting their surrender in battle. Frank Schmidt of 1st Battalion, The Canadian Scottish Regiment (1 CSR) noted the Waffen-SS soldiers' tenacity and fanaticism, while another recruit to the battalion, James Whyte, believed that both sides were particularly desperate to win, most soldiers understanding that a German breakthrough in early June 1944 would mean disaster for the Allies (Veldhoen 2014: 42–43). The battles in Normandy would test different recruitment and training methods as well as the cultural beliefs of the protagonists.

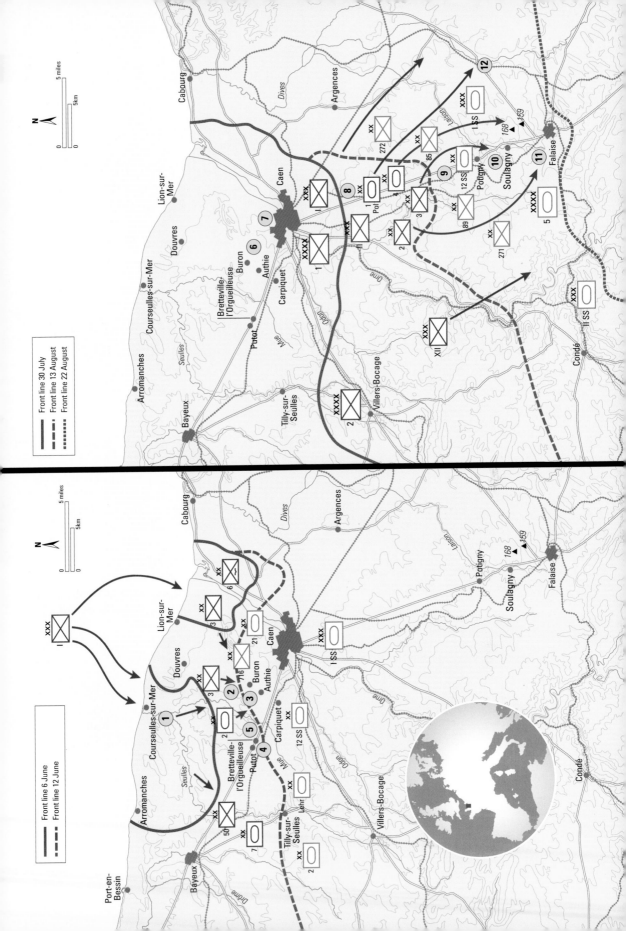

Left map (Front line 6 June / 12 June):

Front line 6 June
Front line 12 June

N
0 5km
0 5 miles

Port-en-Bessin
Arromanches
Courseulles-sur-Mer
Douvres
Lion-sur-Mer
Bayeux
Bretteville-l'Orgueilleuse
Putot
Buron
Authie
Caen
Carpiquet
Tilly-sur-Seulles
Villers-Bocage
Condé
Cabourg
Argences
Dives
Odon
Mue
Seulles
Drôme
Laison
Potigny
Soulagny
Falaise
168
159

1
2
3
4
5
6

xxx
I

xx
6
xx
3
xx
3
xx
16
xx
2
xx
50

O 21
O
O
I SS
O 12 SS
O Lehr
O 7
O 2

Right map (Front line 30 July / 13 August / 22 August):

Front line 30 July
Front line 13 August
Front line 22 August

N
0 5km
0 5 miles

Lion-sur-Mer
Douvres
Courseulles-sur-Mer
Arromanches
Bayeux
Bretteville-l'Orgueilleuse
Buron
Authie
Carpiquet
Putot
Caen
Tilly-sur-Seulles
Villers-Bocage
Condé
Cabourg
Argences
Dives
Odon
Mue
Seulles
Laison
Potigny
Soulagny
Falaise
168
159

7
6
8
9
10
11
12

xxx
I
xxx
1
xxxx
1
xxxx
2
xxx
II
xxx
XII
xxx
II SS

xx 272
xx 85
xx 89
xx 271
xx 3
xx 2

O 4
O 1 Pol
O 12 SS
O 1 SS
O 5

The Opposing Sides

ORIGINS AND DOCTRINE

Canadian

At the start of World War II there was no Canadian military force capable of deploying overseas. The regular army was small, comprising only 4,261 men, and rapid growth was needed. Volunteers were called for and many enlisted. Initially, Prime Minister William Mackenzie King did not want an overseas commitment, but to maintain the support of the public he agreed to recruit a single mobile volunteer division that later expanded into two divisions; by 1941 both were in Britain. The Canadian Government was keen to develop a small but effective armoured force in order to avoid introducing conscription to fill out a larger infantry force, and by the summer of 1943 five divisions

The amount of Canadian combined-arms training varied, with assault units expecting to be withdrawn once the bridgehead was established and receiving limited instruction as the task of getting ashore was prioritized. British doctrine was followed, emphasizing the loose cooperation of units. Tanks were organized into both infantry-support and cruiser brigades, and at first doctrine emphasized direct tank-to-tank combat. Here, a 1 CSR soldier covers the rear of a Churchill tank on exercise in November 1942. (Alex M. Stirton / Canada. Dept. of National Defence / Library and Archives Canada / PA-154302)

(three infantry and two armoured) and two armoured brigades were deployed overseas. Despite this, by early 1943, there was still a shortage of infantry replacements as 12 reserve brigades that legally could not deploy abroad needed personnel, and in March 1944 2,000 recruits had to be mustered from other arms into the infantry. Commanders would seek to minimize casualties during operations, but these ambitions would be frustrated in Normandy. By the end of the war 237,000 personnel had served in the Canadian military with the field force standing at 170,000.

Doctrine emphasized capturing and holding ground rather than exploiting through enemy positions; this approach originated from experiences in World War I when the Germans were quick to organize counter-attacks and in June 1944 would be tested again as the enemy attempted to repel the Allied invasion. Training taught the infantry that holding fire until the enemy was at close range could be effective in stopping attacks from breaking the line; fire discipline needed to be maintained, however, to avoid running out of ammunition. Doctrine also stressed the importance of tanks and artillery, but with time devoted to battle drill, training in combined-arms operations would be limited.

German

Volunteers for the Waffen-SS were sufficient at first, but as the war progressed the demands of the Heer and industry limited numbers. In January 1943 the surrender of the German forces at Stalingrad and the Allied insistence on unconditional surrender of the Axis Powers prompted more stringent policies. That year a 'Culture Day of European Youth' was held that sought to unite Europe against the Soviet Union and

Though the Hitler Youth was not part of the SS, the Waffen-SS always recruited from them, as did all the other German armed services. From 1936 SS weapons trainers and instructors were introduced to Hitler Youth camps. Experienced Waffen-SS veterans of the Eastern Front made recruitment tours to appeal to impressionable Hitler Youth members and encouraged 18-year-olds to join before their call-up to the Wehrmacht. Here (in peaked cap), Gerhard Hein, the *Reichsinspekteur* of Hitler Youth military training camps, is pictured with Waffen-SS volunteers in 1943. Hein was a highly decorated German soldier, being awarded the oak leaves to his Knight's Cross in October 1942. From May 1944 he was a member of the Waffen-SS and in 1945 was an *SS-Obersturmbannführer* commanding a regiment in 12. SS-Panzer-Division *Hitlerjugend*. The Hitler Youth made every effort to appeal to a recruit's interests and set up a Nationalsozialistisches Kraftfahrkorps (National Socialist Motor Corps) that taught 18-year-olds to drive (they could already obtain a motorcycle licence at the age of 16). At the age of 18 members could gain experience driving tanks. (Heinrich Hoffmann/ullstein bild via Getty Images)

This infantryman from 1 CSR is pictured during the Canadian advance towards Hill 168 during the afternoon of 15 August 1944. The Allied offensive in which he is participating, Operation *Tractable*, began the day before and is intended to break through the last German defences north of Falaise. Progress has been good and for the attack on Hill 168 he has been told to expect little resistance. His battalion landed in Normandy on 6 June, since when it has received many replacements. Although he moves towards his objective with the support of a squadron of tanks, Allied artillery support is unusually limited and he is wary that the terrain he is advancing against may hide strong German defences.

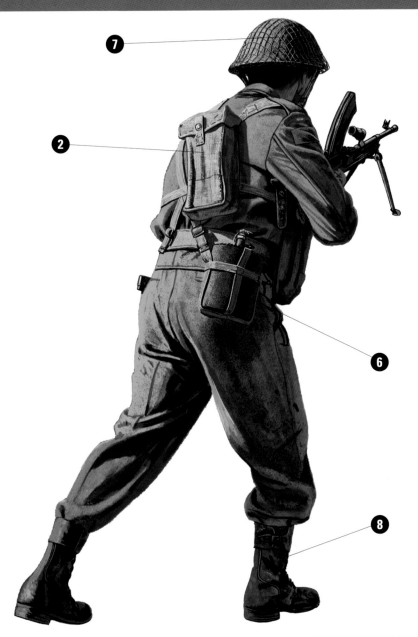

Weapons, dress and equipment

This soldier has a Mk II Bren gun (**1**). Weighing 10.1kg, the weapon had a barrel that could be changed in seconds and utilized magazines, three of which he carries in each of two utility pouches (**2**). The basic pouch carried two magazines. He could fire on the move, but with less accuracy than if the bipod was employed. His loader was responsible for reloading the gun and changing its barrel.

The Canadian Army adopted the battledress uniform (**3**) in September 1939 following assessment and approval of samples sent from the British War Office. Of the same design as those worn by British personnel, Canadian uniforms were made of a higher-quality cloth with metal buttons. They were darker in shade than the British uniforms, with a distinctive green tinge to the dark khaki colour. The gunner wears Pattern 1937 webbing comprising a waist belt (**4**), a pair of braces, a pair of pouches, bayonet and scabbard (**5**), water bottle and carrier (**6**), but he does not wear the small pack. He wears a Mk III helmet with a large-mesh net (**7**) and calf-high boots (**8**). In total, he is carrying approximately 27kg.

German

An order dated 24 June 1943 named the Hitler Youth formation 12. SS Panzergrenadier-Division *Hitlerjugend*; on 30 October it was redesignated a Panzer division. All recruits had to be at least 170cm tall for the infantry and 168cm for other arms. There was not universal enthusiasm to volunteer. In southern Germany the attitude of Hitler Youth members was negative: a recruiter in Dillingen reported that of 185 members born before 30 June 1926, only 30 could be persuaded to volunteer. Many preferred to finish their education or serve with the Reichsarbeitsdienst (Reich Labour Service), but Heer reserve officials complained that coercive measures were being used. Witt investigated in November 1943 and found many instances of personal pressures or compulsory drafting. Klaus Granzow, a Hitler Youth member in a military training camp, recalled that most of those who volunteered to serve in the Waffen-SS opted to join armoured units, and resented the fact that Heer officer cadets like himself had a much harder time of it than the SS recruits (Butler 2003: 43–44). Martin Bormann, the secretary of the Nazi Party, informed Himmler of the growing discontent. SS-Unterscharführer Gustav Tinnacher, recruiting in the notably religious Donauwörth district of Swabia, reported the unpopularity of the SS among the locals, who were shocked by the casualty figures on the Eastern Front (Butler 2003: 65). Also, many Hitler Youth members were serving in other services. For example, 40,000 were recruited into anti-aircraft batteries that defended German cities from Allied bombing; Axmann objected that this was a diversion.

There were many who joined freely. Lothar Eidig, a mechanic, was keen to serve in the vanguard as a motorcycle soldier, and was selected for NCO training; he was heading to 1. SS-Panzer-Division *Leibstandarte SS Adolf Hitler*, but transferred to *Hitlerjugend* because of the latter division's NCO

Indoctrination started when a 10-year-old boy joined the Deutsches Jungvolk. He then moved on to the Hitler Youth aged 14. The Hitler Youth were taught that the state was everything and the individual nothing. The Nazis were trying to convince them that they were born to die for Germany and that war was an ennobling experience. The accomplishments of World War I veterans were lauded in literature. Here, boys are familiarized with the MG 34 machine gun. (ullstein bild/ ullstein bild via Getty Images)

shortage (Peterson 2009: 9). In Eidig's company (15./SS-PzGrenRgt 25) there were nine NCOs who had fought on the Eastern Front. Eidig would be shot in the hand at close range during the attack on Bretteville-l'Orgueilleuse on the night of 8/9 June 1944, with a bullet ricocheting into his abdomen. After being evacuated he was well enough to serve again in September 1944, when he was chosen to attend officer school. He served with 2. SS-Panzer-Division *Das Reich* from March 1945. Otto Funk joined the Deutsches Jungvolk and later the Hitler Youth, earning the shooting and merit badge. He volunteered for *Hitlerjugend* and reported to the Wildflecken training ground on 2 May 1943. Funk served in the same company as Eidig.

There were delays in recruitment, but by May 1944 *Hitlerjugend*'s required strength of 20,516 was reached with a surplus of 2,055 being assigned to 1. SS-Panzer-Division *Leibstandarte SS Adolf Hitler*, at that time based in Belgium for refitting. In June 1944, however, there was a shortage of 2,192 NCOs (out of a required strength of 4,575) and 144 officers (out of 664), despite *Hitlerjugend* establishing an internal NCO course for the 1926 cadre and another (lasting two months) for officer cadets prior to the SS officer course at Bad Tölz. A total of 58 officer cadets were assigned to the officer schools in Germany and would not be available at the time of the Allied invasion of Normandy. From late 1943 the Heer provided 50 mostly specialist officers who served with *Hitlerjugend* in Heer uniform.

WEAPONS, TRAINING AND TACTICS

Canadian

Before the war, there was little experience in the regular Army of command of units larger than a company, no staff planning, and no staff college to develop doctrine. Some officers attended courses in Britain, but there was no combat experience and training suffered. The 51,500 reservists serving at the start of the war trained regularly but lacked equipment. Vehicles were virtually non-existent and weapons were World War I vintage. There were no modern anti-tank or anti-aircraft guns, few Bren guns and mortars, and artillery pieces were obsolete.

Basic training for new recruits who went overseas lasted four months and comprised physical exercise, bayonet practice and rifle training. Unit training up to company level was taught. Eight weeks at a Basic Training Centre common to all arms was followed by eight weeks at an Advanced Infantry Centre. The men were hurried through because numbers were short. In October 1940, 3rd Canadian Infantry Division was called to Debert in Nova Scotia before departure to Britain, but the camp was not finished and the huts lacked electricity and running water. By late 1943, with the camp better established, some battalion-level training was carried out for a month before departure.

Once in Britain, battle drill was taught, comprising high-standard weapons training, intensive physical fitness, field craft, teamwork and familiarization with the battlefield environment. A section practised fire-and-movement tactics and covering fire with weapons available to an infantry company. The aim was to find the enemy, pin him with fire, and then manoeuvre around the

The Bren gun was a light machine gun developed as an accurate weapon that would not squander ammunition. Rate of fire was low, at 500–520rd/min, and the magazine held 30 rounds. Effective range was 550m. Every soldier in the section carried two magazines for the weapon. Here, soldiers with a Bren gun are pictured on exercise in 1943. (Lieut. C.E. Nye / Canada. Dept. of National Defence / Library and Archives Canada / PA-141308)

The Projector, Infantry, Anti-Tank (PIAT) Mk I. Weighing 15kg, the PIAT was an infantry anti-tank weapon that entered service in 1943. A High-Explosive Anti-Tank (HEAT) projectile was fired at 76m/sec by a team of two (gunner and loader). Effective range versus a tank was 110m; buildings could also be targeted out to 320m. To fire the weapon the trigger mechanism had to be cocked, a difficult process that involved standing and twisting the firing pin into position. When a round was fired the spring would be forced back, making reloading not so dangerous. Also, smoke was not emitted when the weapon fired, allowing PIAT teams to retain concealment. (© Royal Armouries PR.1551)

flanks to close for an assault to destroy him. This was done at section, platoon and company level. Responses to a number of different tactical situations were taught on obstacle courses. An emphasis on this type of training taught the infantry to fight as a team, but meant there were fewer opportunities to train with other arms, especially armour.

The section was the basic tactical unit and had two components: a fire group based around the Bren gun, and a group of riflemen to close with the enemy. The rifle team comprised six riflemen armed with the No. 4 Mk 1 Lee-Enfield bolt-action rifle and the section commander armed with a Sten submachine gun. The rifle had a ten-round magazine and an effective range of 500m. The Sten was a Mk II Canadian model that had a 32-round side magazine and an effective range of 100m. The section 2IC, armed with a rifle, commanded the Bren team, comprising a gunner and loader. The company headquarters had two 2in mortars that could fire high-explosive, smoke and illuminating rounds to a range of 460m. The 3in Mk II mortar fielded by the battalion's support company could throw a 4.5kg shell 2,600m; every battalion (each comprising four rifle companies of three platoons each) had six Mk II mortars. In addition to combat tanks, along with six 6-pdr anti-tank guns in the support company, the battalion had Projector, Infantry, Anti-

Tank (PIAT) weapons that the infantry could use. Three were given to each company. Effective range of the PIAT was 110m; a High-Explosive Anti-Tank (HEAT) round was fired that could penetrate 75–100mm of armour at an angle of 90 degrees.

The reliance upon artillery to batter enemy defences was well-established in doctrine. 3rd Canadian Infantry Division had four field regiments equipped with M7 Priest 105mm self-propelled guns; these had a range of 10,425m, lower than the 12,250m range of the British 25-pdrs, because the 105mm shell was heavier. Artillery effectiveness was based around its ability to break enemy morale and keep defenders pinned down rather than destroy their positions; even so, artillery needed to be used intelligently and flexibly in order to support an attack. Brigadier Percy Todd, the commander of all the division's guns, developed an 'Uncle Target', which required all of his artillery to concentrate their fire on a particular target (Milner 2014: 70). In Normandy, the artillery would be used to bombard a target before an infantry advance, but it was more important to fire upon the enemy when he was preparing to mount a counter-attack from the flanks of the advance. Enemy positions that could not be targeted by the battalion weapons were also prioritized. Close air support was frequently available on good-weather days, but suffered some of the same limitations as artillery because targets in cover were difficult to spot.

German

Training the volume of new recruits for *Hitlerjugend* was going to be difficult, and on 4 April 1943 2,000 Hitler Youth leaders born in 1925 reported for a four-week course in 20 *Wehrertüchtigungslager* (WELs; military training camps) to be trained as assistant instructors. They would then help to train recruits before going on to the Waffen-SS NCO School at Lauenburg. On 1 May 1943, 6,000 recruits born in 1926 reported for six weeks of basic military training in the WELs (subsequently shortened to four weeks because of pressures to expedite the division's formation) and another 2,000 were sent

ABOVE LEFT
In February 1944, 3 Anti-Tank Regiment RCA trained with new armour-piercing discarding sabot (APDS) ammunition; these projectiles' higher velocity meant the crews did not have to compensate for the target's speed by aiming ahead of it. The regiment's 4 Bty, 52 Bty and 94 Bty all fielded the 6-pdr Mk 4 anti-tank gun shown here, with 105 Bty equipped with tracked M10 self-propelled guns that mounted a larger 3in gun. At a range of 100m, 142mm of armour was vulnerable to the APDS round; with the more common Armour-Piercing Cap Ballistic Cap (APCBC) round, 92mm of armour was vulnerable. (Lieut. Donald I. Grant / Canada. Dept. of National Defence / Library and Archives Canada / PA-132421)

ABOVE RIGHT
In Bretteville, 3 Anti-Tank Regiment RCA would deploy two batteries: K Tp would be quickly overrun, but G Tp fired effectively, assisted by magnesium flares fired by 2in mortars that highlighted the enemy vehicles. Here, a 6-pdr anti-tank gun crew prepares to fire in Normandy. (Lieut. Ken Bell / Canada. Dept. of National Defence / Library and Archives Canada / PA-137301)

to special military training camps. In a ceremony at Wildflecken training camp that marked their transfer into the Waffen-SS, Axmann spoke of them as the elite of German youth. Once basic training was completed in July 1943, they were then sent to Beverloo training ground in Belgium for a 16-week course and replaced by another 8,000 recruits reporting for basic training.

Despite these measures, in December 1943 Witt reported that the division was not yet fit for an offensive role (Meyer 2005a: 22); individual training was only completed in November 1943 when an order for platoon and company training was promulgated. Recruits were provided with rations that were more substantial than normal and realistic combat scenarios were prioritized instead of drill. Mortars would fire only 45–90m in front of advancing troops. Instructors would detonate a grenade while wearing their helmet to show how the grenades exploded vertically and laterally. Use of firing ranges and forced marches with heavy packs were excluded in favour of weapons practice in open terrain under simulated battle conditions. Ideological training emphasized the damage done to German cities by Allied heavy bombers. Under the guidance of General der Panzertruppen Leo Freiherr Geyr von Schweppenburg (commander of Panzergruppe West), camouflage, radio codes, night-time operations and hand-to-hand combat training were emphasized. Training was hampered because ammunition, tanks and uniforms were all in short supply. Training personnel, especially for heavy weapons, were also lacking. III./SS-PzGrenRgt 25, formed from untrained reserves, was worst off. The commander, SS-Obersturmbannführer Karl-Heinz Milius, was briefly a company commander in France in 1940 where he was wounded. He

then served in training establishments before assuming his appointment in *Hitlerjugend.*

To ameliorate the NCO shortage Witt prioritized the division's NCO course. SS-Sturmmann Jochen Leykauff, a member of 15./SS-PzGrenRgt 25, attended the course and described how Witt inspected their progress. Under Witt's approving eye, Leykauff and his comrades trained using live ammunition and cardboard cut-outs to represent the enemy, then demonstrated their tactical acumen at a sand table before heading outside to discuss tactical problems further (Meyer 2005a: 53). That afternoon a social gathering of instructors and students was held with Witt in attendance.

The Waffen-SS infantrymen were organized into *Züge* (platoons) that each comprised three *Gruppen* of 12 men, each with: two MG 42 machine-gun teams (gunner and loader); the commander, armed with an MP 40 submachine gun; an assistant leader, perhaps with another MP 40 or a rifle; five riflemen; and a driver. The Karabiner 98 kurz was a bolt-action rifle that had an internal magazine capable of holding ten rounds. Effective range was 500m, or 1,000m with telescopic sights. The MP 40 submachine gun had a 32-round magazine with an effective range of 100–200m and a 550rd/min rate of fire. The bipod-mounted MG 42 machine gun could have rounds fed either on a 250-round belt or from two 50-round drum magazines. Effective range was up to 2,000m. An MG 42 machine-gunner would get through on average 100rd/min, though the cyclic rate of fire was 1,200rd/min. The *Kompanie* (three *Züge*) also had two MG 42s mounted on tripods to serve as heavy machine guns, plus two 8cm Granatwerfer 34 mortars that could throw a 3.5kg shell 2,400m at a rate of fire of 15rd/min. The hand-held *Panzerschreck* rocket launcher was also available; it fired HEAT rounds capable of destroying any Allied tank out to 150m. The *Panzerfaust* – a small, disposable tube that fired a high-explosive anti-tank warhead and could be operated by one man – was also used; range was either 30m or 60m depending on the variant.

In a meeting with Hitler on 28 June 1944 Generaloberst Heinz Guderian, Generalinspekteur der Panzertruppen, outlined how traditional German

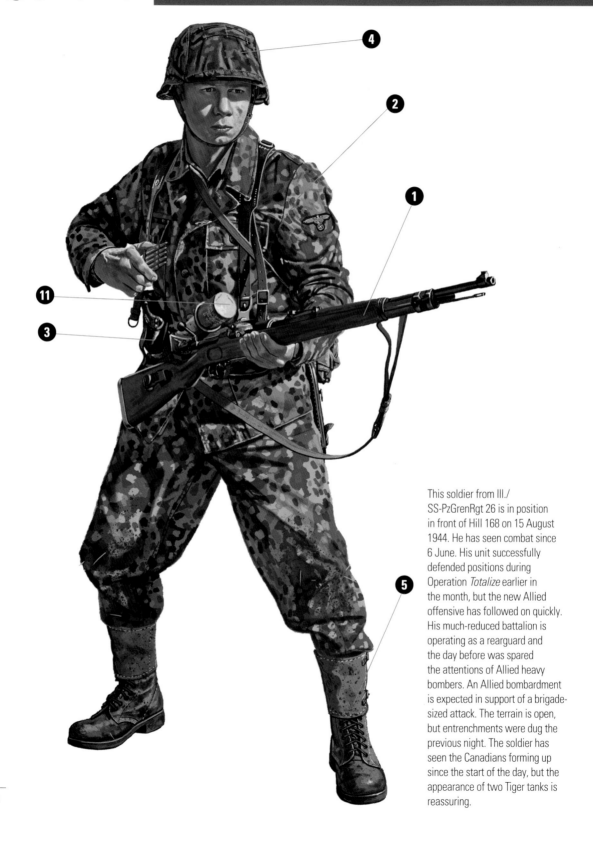

4

2

1

11

3

5

This soldier from III./SS-PzGrenRgt 26 is in position in front of Hill 168 on 15 August 1944. He has seen combat since 6 June. His unit successfully defended positions during Operation *Totalize* earlier in the month, but the new Allied offensive has followed on quickly. His much-reduced battalion is operating as a rearguard and the day before was spared the attentions of Allied heavy bombers. An Allied bombardment is expected in support of a brigade-sized attack. The terrain is open, but entrenchments were dug the previous night. The soldier has seen the Canadians forming up since the start of the day, but the appearance of two Tiger tanks is reassuring.

Weapons, dress and equipment

This soldier's primary weapon is the Karabiner 98 kurz (**1**), a bolt-action rifle with an internal magazine. He is wearing an M44 camouflage tunic (**2**) and trousers. The camouflage pattern was named *Erbsenmuster* ('peas pattern') and was meant to be used in all seasons, dispensing with the need for reversible uniforms. The lightweight, non-reversible jacket pattern printed camouflage design comprised light-green, dark-green, black, dark-brown and light-tan rounded patterns superimposed on contrasting backgrounds.

He has two sets of M1911 ammunition pouches (**3**), each having three pockets holding two five-round clips, making 30 rounds per pouch. His helmet (**4**) has a second-pattern oakleaf camouflage cover with loops that enable foliate cover to be worn. He has puttees and short ankle boots (**5**). A cooking pot (**6**) and water bottle (**7**) are attached to the D-rings on his bread bag (**8**). The gasmask carrier (**9**) was a fluted canister worn over the shoulder on a green webbed strap. The bayonet scabbard and entrenching tool (**10**) share the same housing and he carries an M24 hand grenade (**11**). He has a folded-up *Zeltbahn* (shelter-quarter; **12**) attached to his Y-straps. His equipment weighs approximately 20kg.

By early January 1944, *Hitlerjugend* had received 40 PzKpfw IV Ausf H tanks. Panther tanks only started to arrive in February 1944 and until then their crews undertook drills on foot with flag signals. In early June 1944, exercises with infantry and tanks operating together were planned because new fuel supplies were available. As a result, II./ SS-PzRgt 12, equipped with the PzKpfw IV, had deployed into the area occupied by the *Panzergrenadier-Regimenter* ready for combat. At 0130hrs on 6 June Witt knew the Allied invasion had started. At 0230hrs he alerted his units and at 0400hrs they were ready to move. Here, a *Hitlerjugend* PzKpfw IV crew is having a break during training. (Bundesarchiv Bild 101I-297-1726-17 Foto: Kurth, Bernhard)

combined-arms tactics that sought to break through an enemy line and exploit needed modifying because of the Normandy terrain. He explained that the *bocage* precluded the concentration of German armour and instead required the employment of small armoured units operating in conjunction with infantry, either on foot or mounted in armoured personnel carriers (APCs) (Jentz 1996: 182). Concentrated forces could still be used at night or in bad weather when Allied air supremacy was negated.

Some units would learn these lessons sooner than others. In July 1944 the commander of SS-Panzer-Regiment 2 noted how the new *bocage* tactics meant that Allied artillery was an especially potent threat, making it essential for the Germans to avoid any delays during an attack. In order to target the enemy's artillery positions the attacking force would have to seize any opportunities for exploitation, disregarding any danger to the flanks; the *Panzergrenadiere* would play the chief role in such operations, with the supporting German armour expediting the advance wherever possible. Infantry would attack first, supported by some carried on tanks and others on foot, using some APCs as ammunition carriers but parking the rest in the rear. If the first wave successfully forced the enemy to fall back, the follow-up German armour would undertake the pursuit; if the enemy stood firm, the second wave would renew the attack in different sectors. Each Panzer company would go into action with only 8–12 tanks, with the rest kept as a reserve assault group. Whatever the terrain, tanks were expected to support the infantry and not lead the attack. The closeness of the terrain precluded unified command and independent battlegroups based on reinforced companies would be formed, with each of the *Panzergrenadier-Kompanien* being supported by small groups of tanks (Jentz 1996: 186).

Night-time training was emphasized, even for tanks, which were fitted with headlights that were used only on the orders of the platoon or company commander. The commander of SS-Panzer-Regiment 2 described how headlights would be used sparingly and momentarily; the Panzers would then immediately relocate. Target designation and orders would be issued before the headlights were switched on, at which point all tanks were to fire whether or not they had identified a specific target. The attack would be launched as soon as their firing ceased, with the leading platoons in line abreast, followed by supporting forces in line ahead, ready to counter any threat to the flanks (Jentz 1996: 186). One or two runners on the commander's tank would give alternative means of communication with the infantry.

The Inspektorate der Panzertruppen would codify these lessons into guidelines in August 1944, ordering armoured units to organize as *Panzer-Jagd-Kommandos* or so-called *Panzerkampftrupp* units located immediately behind the front line, subordinated to local *Panzergrenadiere* and ready to counter opposing armour in the event of an enemy breakthrough (Jentz 1996: 189). Alternate positions would serve as *Auflaufstellungen* (positions from which to ambush an adversary at close range, especially from the flank).

COMMAND AND CONTROL

Canadian

Less than half of Canadian Army senior commanders had seen combat and none at the level at which they would exercise command in Normandy. When offensive operations training began, according to the historian Russell A. Hart, orders were inflexible, units were mixed up with each other, march discipline was poor, artillery support was inadequate and tactics were unoriginal. Intelligence gathering, signals procedures and security were all rated as unsatisfactory (Hart 2001: 177). By 1944, training was related to the operational task in Normandy. The Sherbrooke Fusiliers moved in with 1 NNSH in April 1944 and that month in Exercise *Pedal II* practised their role following the landing, namely to move inland on Carpiquet. The infantry rode on the tanks with artillery supporting their advance, but this was from 6 Field Regiment RA as 14 and 19 Field regiments RCA were elsewhere.

Within the infantry battalion radios were provided at company level and functioned at distances up to 8km. The absence of communications between the tanks and infantry (only a small percentage of tanks were equipped with a radio capable of operating on the infantry net) was a persistent problem. Some Shermans had external field telephones that soldiers could use to speak to crewmen, but they had to be with the tank. Tank commanders frequently failed to understand target references described verbally, making the use of smoke or tracer a better method of communication. Battalion commanders had better success liaising with the armoured regiment commander with a No. 19 set.

In September 1943 a memorandum was issued outlining the expected German response to an invasion of Normandy. The area near the River Mue was thought to be ideal tank country and the Canadians expected the Germans to put in a two-division attack either side of the river across

A junior officer gives patrol instructions in Normandy in June 1944. Commanders at company level were well practised in coordinating their personnel. The battle-practice course featured obstacles such as barbed wire and trenches that an entire company had to get over while firing at targets of opportunity. Larger-unit formation training with support arms was carried out and primarily benefited staff officers. (Canada. Dept. of National Defence / Library and Archives Canada / PA-133104)

OPPOSITE

Tank losses in North Africa in 1943 led to an infantry-attacking-first methodology, with armour providing indirect fire support from safe areas, but the attack on Buron and Authie on 7 June 1944 would put tanks at the forefront of the battle. The Sherbrooke Fusiliers acquired Shermans in April and May 1944. None of the crews slated for Normandy had any combat experience and there was a shortage of reserve crews and tanks. The Sherman V that equipped most Canadian armoured units in 1944 had a 75mm M3 gun that could fire an armour-piercing or APDS shell. The armour-piercing round could penetrate 68mm of armour at a 30-degree angle at 455m, falling off to 60mm at 915m. High-explosive and smoke rounds were also used. The M3 gun's muzzle velocity was poor because of the short barrel and a Sherman's armour only protected against a 50mm gun. (Universal History Archive/UIG via Getty Images)

open ground to the harbour at Courseulles-sur-Mer on the day following the landing in order to split the landing forces. This assessment was based on German reports that stated the area north-west of Caen was ideal for armoured warfare (Milner 2014: 45) and that a German counter-attack here would throw the invasion forces into the sea. 3rd Canadian Infantry Division was ordered to secure this area. Issued on 4 March 1944 by British I Corps, Operational Instruction No. 1 stated that two Canadian infantry brigades would establish a line at Putot-en-Bessin–Carpiquet in order to defend the two broad plains either side of the River Mue. The final operational order issued on 5 May reaffirmed the plains' capture to stop probable German counter-attacks. The Canadians' flank would be covered with the capture of Caen by British 3rd Infantry Division.

In early 1944, estimations of the number of Panzer divisions that could reach the beachhead within a week increased to seven, with the Panzer division stationed at Lisieux expected to arrive on the same day as the landings. Allied intelligence detected *Hitlerjugend*'s presence in Lisieux in April and rated the formation as being among the most formidable available to the Germans in France (Milner 2014: 83). In late March, 21. Panzer-Division (thought to have 240 tanks) was detected, but in May it was still believed to be in Rennes with the intention to move to the Cotentin Peninsula rather than Caen. Further inland, 2. and 116. Panzer-Divisionen were assessed as major threats. The other six Panzer divisions in the West were thought to be re-forming, but Schweppenburg later reported that they were all ready to be committed. In May Allied intelligence reported the movement of 21. Panzer-Division and the Panzer-Lehr-Division to

the Normandy area. An Allied intelligence review on 28 May estimated that four Panzer divisions might counter-attack on the day following the landings. There was little that could be done to modify the invasion plan, however. Montgomery correctly thought that most German forces would oppose his formations and not US forces further west.

German

In order to give *Hitlerjugend* combat leadership, a cadre from 1. SS-Panzer-Division *Leibstandarte SS Adolf Hitler* was brought in. Battalion commanders were in their late twenties or early thirties; company and platoon commanders in their early twenties. Leykauff rated himself and his comrades highly in terms of agility and confidence, and trusted the veteran junior leaders who had shared their hardships during training (Meyer 2005a: 54). The relationship between the men and their leaders was close, but draconian punishments were still being used; Witt complained that his subordinates failed to understand that their chief task was to instil SS ideals in the recruits for whom they were responsible (Luther 1987: 63). He ordered platoon and section leaders to share their men's accommodation to demonstrate their concern for their welfare, but some junior NCOs did not know their soldiers well as time was lacking due to the time spent elsewhere on courses. Other units did not have enough NCOs.

The Normandy battlefield environment proved to be particularly difficult for German tanks. During the day they could operate in pairs and use short bounds to move from cover to cover. Firing from hedges was practised; in recognition of the machine gun's key role in the *bocage* terrain, all tanks would receive 5,500 rounds of machine-gun ammunition (Jentz 1996: 186). The PzKpfw IV from II./SS-PzRgt 12 shown here is equipped with a turret-mounted and a hull-mounted machine gun. (Bundesarchiv Bild 101I-297-1722-27 Foto: Kurth, Bernhard)

Radios were distributed from battalion to every company as required. Intelligence of the enemy's movements was good as a special radio monitoring unit (*Nachtrichtennaufklärungszug*) for intercepting enemy radio communications was set up and would improve when a copy of enemy radio procedures and codes was found in a Sherbrooke Fusiliers tank near Authie; also, a coded map of the German defences was found in a Canadian armoured car that was hit on 7 June. The divisional chief-of-staff, SS-Obersturmbannführer Hubert Meyer, explained how, with these discoveries, enemy radio traffic could be evaluated.

The Germans faced the dilemma of whether to hold their Panzers away from the Normandy beaches and prepare a major counter-attack, or to commit them quickly to throw the invaders into the sea. Schweppenburg favoured the former course of action, Generalfeldmarschall Erwin Rommel as commander of Heeresgruppe B in northern France the latter. Hitler gave three Panzer divisions to Schweppenburg (1. SS-Panzer-Division, 12. SS-Panzer-Division and the Panzer-Lehr-Division), as well as 17. SS-Panzergrenadier-Division *Götz von Berlichingen*, and three to Rommel (21., 2. and 116. Panzer-Divisionen), while three remained in southern France. In April 1944, in expectation of an Allied landing on the Normandy beaches, motorized *Hitlerjugend* units were deployed to the area around Lisieux with SS-Panzergrenadier-Regiment 25 furthest west. *Hitlerjugend* was ordered to prepare to advance in three different directions: between the rivers Seine and Somme, between the Seine and the River Orne, and north-west of Caen. Routes were assigned for each eventuality. German units were liable to air interdiction and so to prevent Allied intelligence from finding them, radios were not used. The result was that unit commanders were sometimes unaware of the location of other units.

The tank that equipped I./SS-PzRgt 12, the Panther Ausf A, had a better 7.5cm gun and better armour than the PzKpfw IV Ausf H. The Panther's long gun propelled the round with a high muzzle velocity and could penetrate 111mm of armour at 1,000m. The curved front turret armour was 110mm thick, the sloped front hull 80mm and the sloped side armour 40–50mm. *Schürzen* armour plates were bolted to brackets on the hull side to give better protection. Here are Panthers with their crews relaxing in a Normandy village in 1944. (Bundesarchiv Bild 101I-301-1954-06 Foto: Kurth, Bernhard)

Authie and Buron

7 June 1944

At 1235hrs on 6 June 1 NNSH went ashore at Juno Beach behind the initial assault carried out by 8th Canadian Infantry Brigade; the battalion reached its assembly areas by late afternoon with minimal losses. High tide and the storm surge delayed the landing of many anti-tank guns. The surf was so high that the Universal Carriers towing the 6-pdrs of 3 Anti-Tank Regiment RCA could not land and most would have to wait until the following day, as would 16 tracked M10 self-propelled guns. Also assigned to the Canadians was 62 Anti-Tank Regiment RA, equipped with 48 17-pdr anti-tank guns (two towed batteries and two with M10s); no guns from the regiment slated to support 9th Canadian Infantry Brigade would get ashore in time to participate in the battle in Buron, however. (Gilbert Alexander Milne / Canada. Dept. of National Defence / Library and Archives Canada / PA-132808)

BACKGROUND TO BATTLE

When 3rd Canadian Infantry Division landed in Normandy on 6 June, 9th Canadian Infantry Brigade, including 1 NNSH, was in the second echelon. The brigade's role was to push inland and defend an area north-west of Caen east of the River Mue on ground that was ideally suited to a German armoured counter-attack. At 1820hrs 1 NNSH headed off to Carpiquet airfield on the division's eastern flank with the tanks of Lieutenant-Colonel Mel Gordon's Sherbrooke Fusiliers in support. Major Don Learment

Fuel shortages had held up the Panthers of I./SS-PzRgt 12, which on 7 June were still 50km east of the River Orne, but approximately 50 PzKpfw IV Ausf H tanks of II./SS-PzRgt 12, commanded by SS-Sturmbannführer Karl-Heinz Prinz, would be available at 1000hrs. Here, a *Hitlerjugend* PzKpfw IV is on the move. (Bundesarchiv Bild 101I-297-1725-09, Foto: Kurth, Bernhard)

commanded the advance guard. He had ten 37mm-armed M5 Stuart tanks of the Sherbrooke Fusiliers' reconnaissance unit, commanded by Lieutenant G. Kraus; Captain C.F. Fraser's C Coy, 1 NNSH on 18 carriers of the Carrier Platoon under Captain E. Gray; Lieutenant Couper's No. 9 Platoon from C Coy, 1st Battalion, The Cameron Highlanders of Ottawa (1 CHO), armed with four medium machine guns; M10 self-propelled guns of L Tp, 105 Bty, 3 A/T Regt RCA; one section of 3in mortars; two pioneer sections; and four 6-pdr anti-tank guns from Sp Coy, 1 NNSH. Three other 1 NNSH infantry companies followed, each mounted on a squadron of Sherman tanks. D Sqn, Sherbrooke Fusiliers, dispatched earlier to the east to maintain communication with forces on the flank, was unavailable.

Resistance was encountered at Villons-les-Buissons and Lieutenant-Colonel Charles Petch, realizing he would not make Carpiquet before dark, ordered a halt. The next morning the advance resumed. 7th Canadian Infantry Brigade would keep pace on their right (though the Mue was in the way), and 9th British Infantry Brigade from Sword Beach further east would close in

The *Panzergrenadiere* would benefit from the camouflage uniforms they were wearing that helped them to infiltrate through the wheat fields in front of the position of A Coy, 1 NNSH. Here, Waffen-SS soldiers move towards their objective in Normandy in 1944. (ullstein bild/ullstein bild via Getty Images)

14th Field Group (14 and 19 Field regiments RCA with 79 Medium and 191 Field regiments RA and 3 Bty, 2nd Royal Marine Armoured Support Regiment (2 RMAS) was supposed to support the advance on Carpiquet, but 19 Field Regiment RCA was taking on the heavily fortified radar site at Douvres and only two artillery observers were available. 12th Field Group (12 and 13 Field regiments RCA with 6 Field Regiment RA and 4 Bty, 2 RMAS) was to support 7th Canadian Infantry Brigade at Putot; by 1600hrs on 7 June, 12 and 13 Field regiments RCA were in position on the other side of the River Mue, but would not be called upon by 9th Canadian Infantry Brigade. These personnel from 14 Field Regiment RCA are pictured with their gun on 20 June 1944. (Lieut. Donald I. Grant / Canada. Dept. of National Defence / Library and Archives Canada / PA-131408)

OPPOSITE

Here, an aerial view shows the area between Gruchy (**1**), Buron (**2**) and Authie (**3**) in June 1944. Authie straggled along the north–south road for 500m on a flat plain. A small wood was near the north-west entrance of the village. South of Authie the plain dipped down again to Franqueville (not shown), where the Germans could hide their attacking force and guns. (Laurier Centre for Military Strategic and Disarmament Studies 310/4048)

on the Canadians on the other flank (but was not yet in position because an attack by elements from 21. Panzer-Division towards the coast north-east of Caen had distracted them). If Carpiquet could not be captured, Petch was told to occupy an area of high ground around an 80m contour line south-east of Buron. Before the invasion, intelligence suggested that *Hitlerjugend* would arrive the same day as the landings, but Petch was informed that morning that the Waffen-SS formation was not due until 8 June.

Resistance was not thought to be negligible, however. The Allies realized that the Germans thought the area was valuable as a forming-up area from which to attack the Allied landings. A battlegroup from 21. Panzer-Division, commanded by Oberstleutnant Joseph Rauch and comprising his I./PzGrenRgt 192 plus 2./PzJgAbt 200, 18 self-propelled guns from II./PzArtRgt 155 and two companies from PzPiBtl 220, was placed north-west of Caen. Some elements had advanced to the coast on 6 June but later withdrew to the Buron area. Only in the afternoon was I. SS-Panzerkorps (including *Hitlerjugend*, *Leibstandarte* and the Panzer-Lehr-Division) given to Heeresgruppe B as the German high command thought another landing would occur at Calais and was reluctant to release the Panzer reserves. *Hitlerjugend* was called forward from Lisieux, 80km away. Initially, the division had prepared to move either to Normandy or Calais. SS-PzGrenRgt 25, which had moved north of Lisieux, had to return to Évrecy to move to Normandy. Not until 0900hrs on 7 June did Kampfgruppe *Meyer*, formed around his SS-Panzergrenadier Regiment 25 with elements of II./SS-PzRgt 12 in support, arrive on the reverse slope south of the Bayeux–Caen road; Meyer's force still arrived earlier than Petch was told. An attack with 21. Panzer-Division was planned for 1600hrs. At least SS-Panzergrenadier-Regiment 26, stationed 200km away, would not arrive until late on 7 June.

MAP KEY

1 **0800hrs, 7 June:** Major Learment with C Coy, 1 NNSH and Stuart tanks from the Sherbrooke Fusiliers lead the Canadian infantry battalion. Elements of II./PzArtRgt 155 and two companies from PzPiBtl 220, as well as a replacements battalion from 716. Infanterie-Division, comprise the defences.

2 **0930hrs, 7 June:** The Canadians capture Villons-les-Buissons and the advance on Buron begins.

3 **1150hrs, 7 June:** The Canadians capture Buron despite German shelling from high ground at Saint-Contest. Canadian tanks are targeted by 8.8cm guns. The Canadians fail to establish radio contact with artillery and naval bombardment assets.

4 **1300hrs, 7 June:** Two platoons of C Coy, 1 NNSH commanded by Captain C.F. Fraser advance on Authie and capture the village. One platoon from A Coy, 1 NNSH and three tanks also enter the village, but two tanks are immediately destroyed. Fraser establishes positions in the orchard south of the village.

5 **1420hrs, 7 June:** 5./SS-PzRgt 12 and 6./SS-PzRgt 12 advance from behind the slope at Franqueville. A tank battle erupts and heavy losses are suffered by B Sqn and C Sqn, Sherbrooke Fusiliers.

6 **1530hrs, 7 June:** III./SS-PzGrenRgt 25 attacks Authie from both sides. 1 NNSH elements retreat and some join up with A Coy, 1 NNSH at a hedge line north of the village.

7 **1630hrs, 7 June:** Two platoons of A Coy, 1 NNSH at the hedge line are attacked by German infantry with tank support and surrender when ammunition runs low. B Coy, 1 NNSH is unable to reach the survivors.

8 **1730hrs, 7 June:** The German attack proceeds to Buron where 1 NNSH elements have occupied defensive positions to the north of the village. II./SS-PzGrenRgt 25 has advanced from Bitot in the east, but turns north when the battalion commander, SS-Sturmbannführer Hans Scappini, is killed.

9 **1830hrs, 7 June:** Learment and B Coy elements surrender. The rest of the company, commanded by Captain A. Wilson, are in the anti-tank ditch. D Coy, 1 NNSH holds firm in positions in front of the ditch, assisted by the heavy weapons of Sp Coy behind the anti-tank ditch.

10 **1930hrs, 7 June:** Artillery support is at last available to 1 NNSH. 10 and 16 platoons have surrendered, but an artillery bombardment helps some Canadians to escape.

11 **2000hrs, 7 June:** 1st Battalion, The Stormont, Dundas and Glengarry Highlanders with some guns from 247 Bty, 62 A/T Regt RA are dug in at les Buissons; elements of 1 NNSH retreat into their positions.

12 **2000hrs, 7 June:** The remaining 13 tanks of the Sherbrooke Fusiliers are sent forward and III./SS-PzGrenRgt 25 is forced to retreat from Buron. 1 NNSH elements are unable to occupy the village because of the losses the battalion has suffered.

Battlefield environment

South of Villons-les-Buissons, the countryside was generally an open plain, featuring intermittent stands of trees and small villages, each with its own church, public house, shops and residential buildings (Zuehlke 2005: 88). A flat ridge ran east to west north of Buron and Saint-Contest before dipping down into Buron, which was out of sight from les Buissons but overlooked from Saint-Contest. North of Buron an anti-tank ditch stretched 90m either side of the road and a stone wall stood at the northern perimeter of the village. A road intersection existed in Buron and to the south the road ran 1km into Authie. Between Authie and Buron another road went 1km to Gruchy and then the River Mue. Grain fields were all around, especially to the south and west.

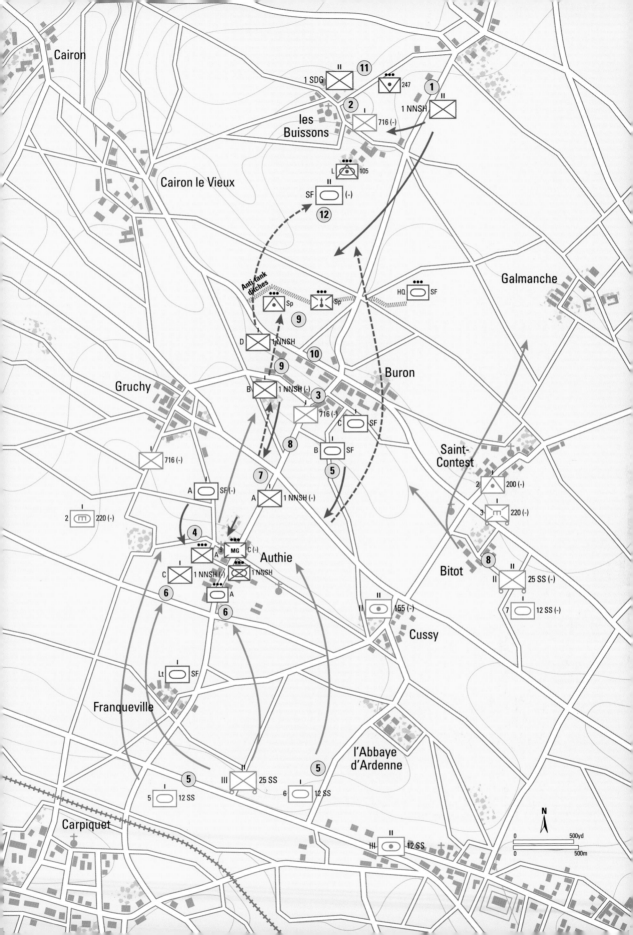

Cairon

les
Buissons

1 SDG ⑪

247 ①

② 716 (-)

1 NNSH

Cairon le Vieux

L 105

SF (-) ⑫

Galmanche

Anti-tank
ditches

Sp ⑨

Sp

HQ SF

D 1 NNSH

⑩

Buron

Gruchy

B 1 NNSH (-) ③

716 (-)

C SF

⑨

⑧

B SF ⑤

716 (-)

Saint-
Contest

A SF (-)

A 1 NNSH (-)

⑦

2 220 (-)

2 200 (-)

3 220 (-)

④

A 9 MG C (-)

Authie

Bitot ⑧

C 1 NNSH (-)

1 NNSH

II 25 SS (-)

⑥

A

7 12 SS (-)

⑥

155 (-)

Cussy

Lt SF

Franqueville

l'Abbaye
d'Ardenne

⑤

III 25 SS

⑤

5 12 SS

6 12 SS

Carpiquet

III 12 SS

N

0   500yd

0   500m

INTO COMBAT

On the morning of 7 June Major Learment was ordered to go straight to Carpiquet and the gun crews of 14 Field Regiment RCA were told to keep pace with the Canadian advance. Naval gunfire support from the Royal Navy light cruisers HMS *Belfast* and HMS *Diadem* was available. At Villons-les-Buissons Learment ran into stragglers from 716. Infanterie-Division, which had provided coastal defence. An 8.8cm gun from 2./PzJgAbt 200 destroyed a light tank on the approach to the village but was mortared, and carriers moved in to approach the gun from the side. By 0930hrs the Canadians had captured the gun and the village.

The Canadians then cleared Buron of German snipers hiding in gardens and alleyways; another 8.8cm gun was destroyed by a tank gun, and a self-propelled gun from II./PzArtRgt 155 was ambushed in a side road with grenades. By about 1150hrs the village was relatively secure. Many Germans surrendered, but Learment noted how the Germans were increasingly opting to resist to the last instead of surrendering or retreating (Zuehlke 2005: 90). Mopping-up operations were handed over to D Coy, 1 NNSH as the Canadian advance guard continued on to Authie.

Major Léon Rhodenizor's A Coy, 1 NNSH, riding on tanks of A Sqn, Sherbrooke Fusiliers, advanced to the west of the Buron road, at first without incident. To the east of the road, the Shermans of B Sqn, Sherbrooke Fusiliers were shelled by 8.8cm guns from higher ground around Saint-Contest. B Coy, 1 NNSH had to dismount and three tanks were lost; Major J. Douglas, OC B Coy, took some time rounding his men up once the shelling stopped. Once the men were gathered together they moved towards Buron on foot. A request for artillery support to fire on Saint-Contest was made to Petch. 14 Field Regiment RCA was 10km away and operating at long range, but Petch's forward observation officer (FOO) told him radio contact had been lost. Allied naval bombardment could have destroyed Saint-Contest, but interference on the air waves prevented the guns being called in.

With no artillery support available, 1 NNSH should have stopped at Buron and waited until the British captured Saint-Contest. Instead, the advance to Authie started, with light tanks covering the open ground to the village and experiencing fire all the way from Saint-Contest and Authie that knocked out several of the vehicles. With covering fire from B Sqn, Sherbrooke Fusiliers and B Coy, 1 NNSH near Buron, Captain Fraser and two platoons of C Coy, 1 NNSH advanced on carriers under light mortar fire and unloaded 45m from the first houses to make the final approach on foot. The third platoon, earlier forced to ground by German shelling, was unavailable. At 1300hrs, Learment radioed that Authie was captured and at 1330hrs stopped for lunch. The carriers probed to Franqueville but were driven away by German mortar fire. Fraser occupied an orchard surrounded by a high hedge covering the approaches to the village from the south and east.

A Coy, 1 NNSH had conducted a sweep of Buron and was deployed west of the village when a bombardment of Authie began. To support Fraser, Rhodenizor sent forward a platoon under Lieutenant L. Sutherland on Shermans of Lieutenant Murray Fitzpatrick's troop of C Sqn, Sherbrooke Fusiliers. His other two platoons occupied a hedge on the right of the Buron–

From the tower at l'Abbaye d'Ardenne the Germans had a good view of the approaching enemy and SS-Sturmbannführer Karl Bartling, the artillery commander located here, assumed command of 21. Panzer-Division's guns as well as his own III./SS-PzArtRgt 12, which had 12 towed 15cm and four towed 10cm guns; he had forward observers with the *Panzergrenadier* battalions. SS-Obersturmbannführer Hubert Meyer, *Hitlerjugend*'s chief-of-staff, was responsible for coordinating the division's approach; here he is in the abbey. (Bundesarchiv Bild 164-14-136, Foto: Woscidlo, Wilfried)

Authie road 500m north of Authie. After Sutherland's men disembarked, two of the tanks were destroyed by 8.8cm fire and Fraser acquired their anti-aircraft machine guns and ammunition. Sutherland's platoon was stationed on the side of the hedge that bordered the main street. The one remaining Sherman belonging to Fitzpatrick was in the orchard but the tank's gun had no turret traverse. Lieutenant Jack Veness and his platoon of C Coy, 1 NNSH had the southern end and half of the other side of the hedge, and Lieutenant John Langley's platoon the rest. The extra Browning machine guns from the two destroyed Shermans were mounted in the hedge on the side away from the town. The historian Marc Milner states that M10 self-propelled guns that belonged to the advance guard were also available.

When the shelling of the village started, the Canadians took cover. Then the light tanks reported enemy armour gathering and Fraser reported their presence to Learment by radio. The Canadian light tanks withdrew, but many were targeted and lost. Gray also sent his carriers to the rear, but remained to see how the situation developed. Lieutenant Couper's 1 CHO machine-gun platoon arrived, but was immediately fired upon. Learment radioed Petch and asked for some artillery. The FOO explained that no artillery was in range, but that naval gunfire could be provided (Zuehlke 2005: 91). Again, radio contact with the ships was lost. Learment was ordered to hold Authie and position himself north of the village at a crossroads. A Coy and B Coy were ordered to close up with him. Gray returned to Buron in his carrier, where D Coy had arrived to support the two platoons of B Coy already there. The battalion, unaware of the approach of Waffen-SS *Panzergrenadiere* and advancing quicker than units on the flanks, was vulnerable and awaited the result of the tank battle.

From l'Abbaye d'Ardenne, SS-Obersturmbannführer Kurt Meyer had observed the Canadian advance during the early afternoon. Beyond Franqueville the ground fell away to Carpiquet and the Germans had plenty of cover while forming up, but when SS-Untersturmführer Karl-Heinz Porsch's

Most 1 NNSH personnel had to dismount from their Sherman tanks because they were targeted by 8.8cm anti-tank guns. The advance proceeded on foot. Here, Canadian infantry pass a German armoured half-track, similar or perhaps the same as those operated by 2./PzPiBtl 220. (Ken Bell / Canada. Dept. of National Defence / Library and Archives Canada / PA-132888)

platoon from 5./SS-PzRgt 12 reconnoitred north towards Authie he lost three tanks to Shermans of A Sqn, Sherbrooke Fusiliers in a surprise encounter. Meyer could wait no longer and ordered an immediate attack. At 1420hrs SS-Obersturmbannführer Max Wünsche, the commander of SS-Panzer-Regiment 12, contacted two companies (5./PzRgt 12 and 6./PzRgt 12) by radio, ordering them to advance. His command tank was in the monastery's grounds with communication wire laid from the spire to the tank.

A tank battle erupted on both sides of Authie and lasted two hours. Major G. Mahon's B Sqn, Sherbrooke Fusiliers was advancing towards the high ground when German tanks suddenly appeared at the top of the rise. Captain Merritt Bateman, 2IC B Sqn, was soon targeted and one hit blew him out of his tank, which was turned into a burning wreck. He went over to another tank to resume command. Lieutenant N. Davies stopped two German tanks with his 17-pdr gun (Zuehlke 2005: 104). With his radio out of action, Davies stood up out of his turret and waved to three other tanks to withdraw to les Buissons behind 1 NNSH. His Sherman was hit and most of the crew baled out with their wounded commander. Only five tanks remained from the 11 with which B Sqn had started the day. Many were targeted by 8.8cm guns as well as by German tanks. C Sqn, Sherbrooke Fusiliers went to help, but its tanks were also targeted by the 8.8cm guns and only six escaped.

Seeking to occupy the high ground between Buron and Authie, Petch ordered B Coy to advance to A Coy's position despite the lack of cover there. A hedge was reached, but offered no shelter, and with casualties mounting Douglas decided to withdraw. Ordered to try again, Douglas went forward to discuss coordination with Rhodenizor, but was wounded while returning to bring up his men. Captain Wilson assumed command of B Coy and was told by Petch to advance in carriers. The advance broke down north of Authie due to mortar fire and the men retreated into Buron. The Canadian FOOs withdrew to the anti-tank ditch north of Buron.

At Authie Veness was told to bring up a shot-up 1 CHO carrier that was on the northern side of the village. The vehicle, with a medium machine gun on board, was placed on the orchard hedge with a good field of fire. Fraser was trying to use a tank radio to talk to Petch as the company No. 18 set was damaged. Then, at around 1530hrs, the Germans launched an attack from both sides of Authie. The Germans deployed III./SS-PzGrenRgt 25 into attack formation with two companies up and one in reserve (9., 10. and 11.). Hubert Meyer does not record whether 12. (Schwere) Kompanie participated. The Waffen-SS men covered 1,200m of open ground on foot without being targeted by Allied artillery. Elements of Oberleutnant Fritsch's 9./SS-PzGrenRgt 25 took advantage of folds in the ground and the wheat fields to retain some degree of concealment. Nine tanks supported their advance. The *Panzerpioniere* in half-tracks provided support from the west.

Canadian machine guns taken from the carrier and the tanks cut down many Germans. The turret of the damaged Sherman in the orchard managed to traverse slightly and fire high-explosive rounds. The German artillery barrage initially descended on the village buildings, but the FOO of 9./SS-PzArtRgt 12 radioed for the orchard to be targeted. Almost immediately, according to Will Bird, whose son Captain Stephen Stanley Bird fought in the battle, German artillery pummelled the orchard, but the Canadian machine guns continued to target the Germans (Zuehlke 2005: 107). Noting that fire was coming from a different direction, Veness turned round to see Sutherland's men being overrun and the Germans pushing into the field next to the orchard. 11./SS-PzGrenRgt 25 had infiltrated around to the west of Authie. SS-Sturmmann Karl Vasold of 9./SS-PzGrenRgt 25 described how his company managed to get into the village where the first house-to-house combat took place. Withdrawal to the north side was the only option for the Canadian defenders. The wounded remained behind to give covering fire. Smoke filled the streets and assisted Veness to escape; with a group of men he dashed down alleyways and, pushing aside small groups of the enemy, reached the village limits. Now 45m of open ground and then 180m of grain separated them from the hedge where A Coy, 1 NNSH lay. Half of the Canadian section was cut down by a German tank, but Veness reached the hedge with the rest. Langley could not get away and with three men supporting him was shot and killed. Sutherland saw Fraser, who had ordered those that could to try to escape, share the same fate.

According to Bird, the Sherman in Authie stopped three German tanks before exploding in flames. Milner says that the Sherman's gun was not working, but the historian Mark Zuehlke says that the gun did indeed fire and destroyed three tanks. Milner makes no mention of the fate of the tank or the loss of the German armour. There is a reference in the 1 NNSH War Diary that says the gun on Fitzpatrick's tank was not working, making the German losses unlikely. Regimental records of SS-Panzer-Regiment 12 show that only seven of the tanks from the two companies that were deployed against Authie were lost in total on 7 June (though according to SS-Sturmmann Hans Fenn, a gunner with I. Zug, 6./SS-PzRgt 12, double this number had damage that

Escaping from Authie

This scene depicts the moment elements of A Coy and C Coy, 1 NNSH retreated from Authie during the early afternoon of 7 June. German infantry and tanks were all around and close encounters were experienced. For example, Corporal Douglas Wild and his men, initially with Lieutenant Sutherland, were targeted by two German tanks. Wild jumped over a hedge where moments before a shell had killed Corporal Gordon Holm and then a building collapsed into the road. When the dust cleared he found himself behind a German tank and ran up a side alley, into three German soldiers in single file. The leader went at him with a bayonet, which Wild parried and then he shot the other two. He threw two smoke grenades and crossed a street with Germans taking shots at him from upper-storey windows. This illustration shows a group of soldiers crossing the road near the church in order to reach a wooded area bordered by a stone wall that is north-west of the village. The 1 NNSH personnel have surprised the first two soldiers of a Waffen-SS patrol advancing along a winding road towards the church. A PzKpfw IV is turning into the road, but has not noticed them and is heading away from the Canadians.

put them out of action), and some losses may have occurred at Authie. The M10 self-propelled guns were all participating in the battle at Buron and none was lost, suggesting that they were not present in Authie and could not have caused the German losses. Fitzpatrick survived the battle, but his tank was almost certainly lost.

Other German tanks careered into the village, with some crashing into the stone buildings. Sutherland organized his men to dash across the main street, but when he made the attempt a shell exploded in a house by the road. He survived and took his men on a wide detour that nearly reached Gruchy before turning in on Villons-les-Buissons. Sergeant Bill Gammon was separated from Sutherland, but in the smoke managed to cross the road and run into two Germans in a lane. He shot one with his Sten submachine gun and when the weapon malfunctioned smashed the other in the head. He made his way to battalion positions that evening. Private F. Wallace ducked up an alley and found himself behind seven German soldiers. Some shells exploded and Wallace ran through the smoke and noticed another member of his battalion darting up a passageway. Wallace followed and joined up with Sutherland. Sergeant Earl McKillop and his brother Walter were taken prisoner, but exploding shells pinned down their captors and they made a successful dash for freedom, escaping into the tall wheat. Bleeding badly, Lance Corporal William MacKay was forced to surrender; having anticipated a rapid victory, his captors were furious with the Canadians (Zuehlke 2005: 109).

Three companies of III./SS-PzGrenRgt 25 – 9. (Oberleutnant Fritsch), 10. (Oberleutnant Joachim Dietrich) and 11. (SS-Obersturmführer Georg Stahl) – plus 5. and 6./SS-PzRgt 12 then moved to attack Buron, supported by fire from III./SS-PzArtRgt 12 and perhaps the heavy weapons of 12./SS-PzGrenRgt 25 (SS-Obersturmführer Wörner). A heavy-infantry-gun platoon from 13./SS-PzGrenRgt 25 also accompanied the battalion. At Buron Petch had moved one platoon of B Coy into German trenches to the north of the village and the other two platoons into the anti-tank ditch to provide all-round defence in order to fight to the finish. Learment with the remaining platoon from C Coy was also in the entrenchments north of Buron. The anti-tank ditch proved immensely useful as the men could move concealed within

the entrenchment rather than be forced to rely on isolated shell scraps. Major Cy Kennedy with D Coy occupied positions to the north of the village and endured an artillery barrage that killed Captain Harold Longley, 2IC D Coy. Lieutenant Harold Murphy's 16 Platoon was slightly in advance of the rest of the company. Fields of fire were severely limited due to the grain. Lieutenant Charles MacDonald also arrived with the battalion mortars that were placed behind the anti-tank ditch. Regimental Sergeant Major McNeill took charge of the evacuation of wounded in carriers and then joined D Coy. Most of Buron was abandoned.

At the hedge near Authie Rhodenizor, with 50–60 men, realized B Coy would not arrive. They viewed with trepidation the events at Authie and noticed the daring escape of Veness and a handful of men. The ground was hard and the shell scraps the men were taking cover in provided scant protection. Six German tanks appeared in a line on the right and staying out of PIAT range targeted their positions, killing nine men from Lieutenant G. Smith's platoon. German infantry assaulted forward, but were blasted at close range. The company withstood attacks for an hour, but ammunition ran low and the carrier with the reserve rounds was blown up. The radio could not receive any messages, but could still send. German tanks raked the area with machine-gun bullets and high-explosive rounds exploded. As Lieutenant Jack Fairweather loaded ammunition from a broken Bren gun into a rifle, Germans appeared from the wheat fields and Captain Joseph Trainor surrendered. Standing up to see what was going on, Rhodenizor was captured and taken prisoner, as was Company Sergeant Major R. Adair (Zuehlke 2005: 112). A German machine-gunner shot two men who had their hands up; Private W. Gerrior, still hidden in the grain and seeing what had occurred, shot the two manning the gun and three others before removing the bolt of

At the hedge north of Authie Captain Joseph Trainor, 2IC A Coy, 1 NNSH, went round the positions, encouraging the men. Lieutenant Jack Fairweather, a platoon leader, redistributed Bren gun ammunition, but rates of fire fell as ammunition ran out. The Germans were close and an occasional grenade arced over the hedge to shower shrapnel on the defenders. Here, a Bren gunner of 1 HLIC can be seen in Normandy in June 1944. (Lieut. Ken Bell / Canada. Dept. of National Defence / Library and Archives Canada / PA-131432)

his rifle. The Germans gathered up the other company members and three were shot by pistol while they were marched along. The prisoners were taken to Authie and witnessed more murders as the Germans realized the extent of their losses. Major Rhodenizor spoke fluent German and persuaded some of the captors to relent.

Three companies of II./SS-PzGrenRgt 25 – 5., 6. and 7. (8. (Schwere) Kompanie had not arrived) – were then committed from Bitot in the east. Sent out to observe the eastern approaches to Buron, Major Sydney Radley-Walters with three tanks from C Sqn noticed German infantry and fired at them with machine guns; the battalion commander, SS-Sturmbannführer Hans Scappini, was killed while accompanying 7./SS-PzGrenRgt 25. Radley-Walters then waited until German tanks approached to within 700yd (640m) and then fired at them with his gun. Hubert Meyer stated that the battalion's focus was not Buron but Galmanche and Malon and their involvement in the attack on Buron was probably limited, though Milner suggests that they forced Learment out of his positions east of the road entrance to Buron.

With artillery support, III./SS-PzGrenRgt 25 advanced into positions north-west of Buron. Many of the defenders were pinned down by the bombardment and the high stand of grain obstructed their view. Tanks also approached Buron and a PzKpfw IV was targeted by Corporal Roy Noonan. He stood up out of the grain and fired a Bren gun; the tank driver swerved, bringing the PzKpfw IV into the line of sight of Noonan's anti-tank gun. The tank was destroyed.

At 1830hrs Learment, with a platoon, realized his flank was turned. Machine guns targeted the Canadian positions and pinned them down. An SMG-armed Waffen-SS soldier moved into view and demanded that Learment surrender, only to be shot, giving the Canadian a chance to reload his Bren gun. The weapon failed to fire, however, and this time there was no alternative. Learment surrendered and with ten Nova Scotians was lined up against a wall, but at the last moment a German sergeant ran up and ordered the Waffen-SS men not to shoot. Learment and his men were repeatedly punched and kicked during a search. Then one of the Germans noticed a grenade dangling from Private John Metcalfe's webbing belt. He shot Metcalfe in the back with his SMG, knocking him off his feet; the German then shot him in the head, while the other Waffen-SS soldiers continued to search the prisoners. Learment was brought to l'Abbaye d'Ardenne where Meyer questioned him; later, ten men (four of 1 NNSH and six tankers) were randomly chosen for questioning by military police. Along with a wounded Nova Scotian they were then shot in the head or bludgeoned to death. Learment and the remaining 100 prisoners were marched out and a truck deliberately ran into them, killing two men (Zuehlke 2005: 115–16).

By 1930hrs, B Coy, 1 NNSH – with some 1 CHO machine guns commanded by Major Roger Rowley, 2IC 1 CHO – were running low on ammunition and had been ordered to evacuate their positions in the anti-tank ditch and move to les Buissons. D Coy could not pull out and had to endure repeated attacks. Behind the ditch to the right of the road the battalion mortars were firing in support. With ammunition expended, the platoon mounted carriers and also retreated to les Buissons where they found 1st Battalion, The Stormont, Dundas and Glengarry Highlanders (1 SDG). Then Allied artillery

at last started firing. The 1 NNSH War Diary described how 16 Platoon ran out of ammunition; surrounded, they were forced to surrender, but elements of the platoon escaped during an Allied artillery bombardment, making their way back to the Canadian lines (Meyer 2005a: 144). Petch asked Gordon to send forward the 13 remaining tanks deployed behind a wood at les Buissons. When German tanks started to withdraw their infantry was vulnerable and the Sherbrooke Fusiliers War Diary described how the German foot soldiers were quickly overrun (Meyer 2005a: 144–45). SS-Rottenführer Paul Hinsberger, a medical orderly in III./SS-PzGrenRgt 25, recalled how the severely wounded of both sides were carried aboard the withdrawing German tanks (Meyer 2005a: 143). Shermans took off in pursuit, chasing the Germans to Authie.

Despite the German retreat, the Canadians could not hold Buron as there was insufficient infantry and permission was given for a withdrawal to Villons-les-Buissons that night. Sutherland and his platoon sergeant, F. Poynter, reported the defence of Authie. In all, 35 men from A Coy and C Coy got out; 60 men from B Coy and 70 from D Coy also retreated successfully. Losing 84 killed, 30 wounded and 128 taken prisoner (including 21 wounded), 1 NNSH had endured a grim introduction to combat. A total of 37 Canadians who surrendered in Authie were executed, many on a whim, sometimes by officers starting the shooting. Also, 22 tanks from the Sherbrooke Fusiliers were destroyed, with six more badly damaged; 26 tankers were killed and 34 wounded. Learment would escape while being transported on a rail car. Veness and Fairweather also escaped from the train.

Hubert Meyer suggests that 5. and 6./SS-PzRgt 12 certainly had nine destroyed tanks and suffered 13 killed and 11 wounded. Mark Zuehlke states that 31 tanks were lost, but many were in fact self-propelled guns from II./PzArtRgt 155. III./SS-PzGrenRgt 25 suffered 28 dead, 70 wounded and 12 missing. On 8 June the Germans reoccupied Buron with 9., 10. and 12./SS-PzGrenRgt 25 and a supporting platoon of PzKpfw IV tanks. They fortified the village with trenches, minefields, barbed wire and anti-tank ditches. The new German commander was Hauptmann Fritz Steger, a Heer officer.

ABOVE LEFT
Anti-tank guns deployed at les Buissons started firing when the Germans advanced around Buron. SS-Sturmmann Hans Fenn, a gunner with I. Zug of 6./SS-PzRgt 12 described how his platoon abruptly came under Canadian anti-tank fire in the open (Meyer 2005a: 141). Fenn's tank was hit in the side while trying to turn away. Here, a destroyed PzKpfw IV is inspected after Buron had been captured on 8 July. (Lieut. H. Gordon Aikman / Canada. Dept. of National Defence / Library and Archives Canada / PA-162728)

ABOVE RIGHT
On the radio Major Cy Kennedy heard German misinformation, with spoof orders in English (a radio had fallen into German hands), including a message to retreat. He asked for a bombardment on his positions. Here, Kennedy is depicted with Lieutenant-Colonel Charles Petch (with binoculars). (Lieut. Ken Bell / Canada. Dept. of National Defence / Library and Archives Canada / PA-133733)

Bretteville-l'Orgueilleuse

8–9 June 1944

BACKGROUND TO BATTLE

Lieutenant-Colonel Foster Matheson's 1st Battalion, The Regina Rifle Regiment (1 RRR), belonging to 7th Canadian Infantry Brigade (Brigadier Harry Foster), experienced tough resistance clearing the beaches at Courseulles-sur-Mer on 6 June. By 2200hrs the battalion dug in, having advanced 11km. 100 reinforcements arrived to make up for losses suffered during the assault, mostly in A Coy, whose commander was wounded and replaced by Captain Ron Shawcross. The battalion's objective was the high ground near Bretteville-l'Orgueilleuse on the Caen–Bayeux road.

At 0730hrs on 7 June 1 RRR moved off, captured the undefended village at midday, and prepared positions as a German counter-attack was assessed as likely. The battalion was the first to gain its objectives, which meant it was exposed, especially to the east when 1 NNSH was thrown out of Authie and vacated Buron. Matheson deployed his companies in an arc of isolated positions from Norrey to Rots. Located on a hill with good lines of sight to any approaching enemy, Norrey was occupied by C Coy. B Coy was in Rots, 2.5km east of Bretteville; D Coy was in la Villeneuve to guard the bridges over the River Mue; and A Coy was in Bretteville as battalion reserve. Further west, 1st Battalion, The Royal Winnipeg Rifles (1 RWR) occupied broken countryside around Putot-en-Bessin. On 8 June Foster's brigade, deployed in a narrow salient, was placed on the defensive. Foster managed to obtain two 1 CHO platoons, several batteries of 3 Anti-Tank Regiment RCA, and two batteries of 17-pdr guns from the British 62 Anti-Tank Regiment RA.

Rommel had ordered an attack by three Panzer divisions on 8 June, but the Panzer-Lehr-Division was still arriving and 21. Panzer-Division was fighting defensive battles. SS-Obergruppenführer Josef 'Sepp' Dietrich, the commander

Here, the area around Bretteville-l'Orgueilleuse to the north (**1**) and Norrey to the south (**2**) is visible, as well as Cardonville Farm to the west (**3**). (Laurier Centre for Military Strategic and Disarmament Studies)

During the afternoon of 8 June, Witt arrived at l'Abbaye d'Ardenne and Meyer explained to him a plan to shorten the line that comprised a high-speed night attack by armour on Rots and Bretteville while Mohnke would attack Norrey. Wünsche would accompany the attack as the headquarters tanks of II./SS-PzRgt 12 had not turned up; here, in camouflage uniform, Wünsche is talking with Witt. (Bundesarchiv Bild 146-1984-031-19A Foto: Woscidlo, Wilfried)

OPPOSITE

Cardonville Farm to the south comprised a two-storey farmhouse with 60cm-thick stone walls, plus barns, storage sheds and yard. A 2.5–3m-thick wall extended from the house around some outbuildings and barns; an orchard was on the north side and the railway line on the south. Here, an aerial photo shows the farm. (Laurier Centre for Military Strategic and Disarmament Studies 310/4034)

of I. SS-Panzerkorps, had only *Hitlerjugend* to comply with the order. SS-Obersturmbannführer Kurt Meyer's SS-Panzergrenadier-Regiment 25 was occupied, but SS-Obersturmbannführer Wilhelm Mohnke's SS-PzGrenRgt 26, travelling to the front on 7 June, was available. Before dawn on 8 June Witt ordered I./SS-PzGrenRgt 26 to attack Norrey and II./SS-PzGrenRgt 26 to attack Putot, with III./SS-PzGrenRgt 26 to move behind the latter. I./SS-PzRgt 12 would not reach the battlefield until the evening.

At 0300hrs on 8 June, I./SS-PzGrenRgt 26 launched the attack on Norrey, but was severely hampered by Allied artillery and mortar fire for much of the day (Meyer 2005a: 165). 13 Field Regiment RCA fired 976 rounds between 1800hrs on 7 June and 0600hrs the next day. SS-Obersturmführer Düwel was wounded and could not call in fire support because Canadian radio transmitters were breaking his signal. II./SS-PzGrenRgt 26 arrived late and attacked at 0830hrs, and was successful despite losses (98 casualties). Suffering 265 casualties, 1 RWR was rendered combat ineffective and was pulled from the line and placed in reserve, but a counter-attack by 1 CSR retook Putot that evening.

As German tanks from I./SS-PzRgt 12 were observed during the day, Matheson thought the Germans would launch an armoured attack that night, but from the south or south-west. B Coy (Captain John Treleaven) moved from Rots to the east side of Bretteville. Foster hoped to make the brigade fortress secure by pulling closer to Bretteville. In the village were A Coy, B Coy and battalion HQ with 6-pdr anti-tank guns and medium machine guns. C Coy (Major Charles 'Stu' Tubb) remained in Norrey; Foster had wanted the company out as the position was exposed, but Matheson refused. Two batteries of 17-pdr anti-tank guns from 62 Anti-Tank Regiment RA deployed behind Bretteville. D Coy, comprising 80 all ranks, occupied Cardonville Farm, north-west of Norrey; the company was commanded by Captain Gordon Brown, the battalion's transport officer, as Major John Love had been killed and the 2IC wounded on 6 June.

The Panzer-Lehr-Division moved west to recapture Bayeux late on 8 June; *Leibstandarte* and 116. Panzer-Division were released for service in Normandy and began to move on 9 June. 12. SS-Panzer-Division still needed to capture the start line for the attack along the River Mue. Some 6.4km separated III./SS-PzGrenRgt 25 at Buron and I./SS-PzGrenRgt 26 at Saint-Manvieu. If SS-Panzergrenadier-Regiment 26's right flank moved north to Rots the line could be reduced by 3.5km. Also, a move along Route Nationale 13 to Bretteville would encircle Norrey. Meyer and Wünsche discussed the details and agreed that the Panther battalion, I./SS-PzRgt 12, would lead the attack, alongside the reconnaissance troops of SS-Hauptsturmführer Horst von Büttner's 15./SS-PzGrenRgt 25. They would be supported by two companies of I./SS-PzRgt 12 with 26 Panthers, as only SS-Hauptsturmführer Hans Pfeiffer's 4./SS-PzRgt 12 and SS-Hauptsturmführer Kurt Berlin's 1./SS-PzRgt 12 had arrived. Mohnke agreed to commit I./SS-PzGrenRgt 26 from Saint-Manvieu to approach Bretteville from south and south-west of Norrey on the basis that Cardonville Farm was secured; there was no wireless link between Meyer and Mohnke, however, and coordination was almost non-existent.

1 2220hrs, 8 June: 15./SS-PzGrenRgt 25 motors into Rots and pushes on to Bretteville, accompanied by 4./SS-PzRgt 12 either side of the road and 1./SS-PzRgt 12 to the south of the road.

2 2230hrs, 8 June: Panthers start shelling B Coy, 1 RRR in Bretteville; the initial German infantry attack, mounted by 15./SS-PzGrenRgt 25, is repulsed.

3 0030hrs, 9 June: A Panther is knocked out in front of battalion headquarters in Bretteville. 1./SS-PzRgt 12 is ordered to move around Bretteville to the south.

4 0130hrs, 9 June: 15./SS-PzGrenRgt 25 attacks Bretteville again. Some time later, SS-Untersturmführer Reinhold Fuss (an infantry platoon leader) and six German soldiers enter the church.

5 Early hours, 9 June: Panthers enter Cardonville Farm and are surprised by D Coy, 1 RRR. A Canadian platoon in positions outside the farm compound is destroyed, but the remainder are safe in the buildings.

6 Early hours, 9 June: The Panther attack against the southern side of Bretteville fails. 1./SS-PzRgt 12 retreats.

7 c.0400hrs, 9 June: 4./SS-PzRgt 12 pulls out from the eastern side of Bretteville.

8 0445hrs, 9 June: The German battlegroup withdraws from the vicinity of Bretteville. The Panthers at Cardonville Farm also withdraw.

9 c.0600hrs, 9 June: 2./SS-PzGrenRgt 26 attacks Cardonville Farm, but is repulsed when artillery targets the company.

Battlefield environment

According to Brigadier Foster, the open terrain around Bretteville-l'Orgueilleuse was studded with many villages, most located in the areas closer to sea level; the Germans made good use of the observation and targeting opportunities offered by possession of the higher ground (Zuehlke 2005: 150).

Bretteville would be largely destroyed; here, the results of artillery bombardments and the direct fire from the Panthers' guns are clearly visible in the village. (Canada. Dept. of National Defence / Library and Archives Canada / PA-133735)

Rots

26 SS
A

La Villeneuve

River Mue

1

8

15
II

15
III

Sp

1 RRR

MG
A

15
I

2

12 SS
4

7

12 SS
1

3

Bretteville-
l'Orgueilleuse

1 RRR
B

4

94
3

3

HQ
1 RRR

94
G

1
I

III
1

Norrey

26 SS
3

1 RRR
C

A
I
1 RRR

Sp

II
1

1
I

Sp
1 RRR

9

26 SS
2

5

D
1 RRR

6

Cardonville Farm

Sp

Sp
E

246
I

62 (-)

N

500yd
500m

0
0

INTO COMBAT

At 2120hrs on 8 June SS-Obersturmbannführer Kurt Meyer, with a section of motorcycle troops behind him, led the Panthers and 15./SS-PzGrenRgt 25 over the bridge at la Villeneuve that D Coy had not destroyed. During training at Beverloo Meyer had promised the company he would accompany them in their first combat. SS-Oberscharführer Helmut Belke would drive the motorcycle that took Meyer into battle. According to Meyer, the soldiers were worried that he was too exposed in his motorcycle. The majority of Büttner's company were riding on the tanks. As the leading Panther travelling along the road approached Bretteville, a well-camouflaged tank (probably a Sherman used by a FOO from 2 RMAS) appeared. Both tanks stopped and exchanged gunfire. The Sherman fired first, but the round bounced off the Panther's front. Surprisingly, the Panther's first round had no effect, but the second round sent the Sherman's turret into the air.

The two Panthers in the lead resumed the advance and stopped a few hundred metres from Bretteville at the top of a slope. They had already overrun a carrier section and two medium machine guns on the crest. Their approach was not observed from the village because of the ridge, but, as SS-Sturmmann Hans Kesper, driver of a Panther in Pfeiffer's IV. Zug, described it, amid fierce anti-tank fire from 6-pdrs of 94 Bty, 3 A/T Regt RCA, the tank ahead of his own was hit. While still outside the village, SS-Untersturmführer Reinhold Fuss, an infantry platoon leader, ordered his men to disembark and continue the advance on foot (Meyer 2005a: 179–80).

B Coy had observed the Germans approaching down the road from la Villeneuve and opened fire. Prearranged artillery barrages also began falling. German infantry scrambled off the tanks and advanced bound by bound using ditches as cover. Meyer tried to drive a motorcycle into the village to reach them, but the fuel tank was hit and set on fire. Several soldiers rolled him in the muddy ditch by the side of the road to quench the flames on his uniform and he remained uninjured. Then Büttner was hit and Meyer

Serving in III. Zug, 15./SS-PzGrenRgt 25, SS-Sturmmann Otto Funk was the machine-gun loader for SS-Sturmmann Klaus Schuh, and rode into battle on SS-Hauptsturmführer Hans Pfeiffer's Panther (Peterson 2009: 41). Once through the narrow streets the Germans fanned out into wedge formation with two Panthers from 4./SS-PzRgt 12 (including Pfeiffer's) in front and the platoons staggered either side of the road. 1./SS-PzRgt 12 was in the high wheat fields to the south of the road. (Keystone-France/Gamma-Keystone via Getty Images)

called over Dr Stift to dress the wound. Belke gave covering fire and shot a Canadian that dashed across the road, but was soon fatally wounded by a bullet. A tank commanded by SS-Unterscharführer Friedrich Hartmann was hit in the turret and put out of action. Pfeiffer ordered his tanks to shoot at the buildings to illuminate the situation. An order from Wünsche ordered Pfeiffer to advance into Bretteville. At midnight, with Pfeiffer's I. Zug leading, two Panthers drove up the main road. Matheson was in a trench behind a house and observed them entering the village. The Panthers' main guns started firing and their machine guns rattled, and many buildings collapsed in flame and smoke.

At the same time as the attack on Bretteville, I./SS-PzGrenRgt 26 moved against Norrey. Tubb recalled that the sound of voices in the dark betrayed the presence of the enemy near le Mesnil-Patry; two Bren gun teams from 13 Platoon ambushed the Germans and prompted their rapid withdrawal (Zuehlke 2005: 197). 79 Medium Regiment RA also targeted them.

In Bretteville the lead Panther had reached the front gates of the courtyard by Matheson's headquarters, raking the area with machine-gun fire. Rifleman Joseph Lapointe fired a PIAT at the Panther's side armour from 14m, but the tank continued on and unintentionally set off some Type 75 anti-tank grenades, breaking the right track. A second PIAT round missed, but a third hit the Panther and caused the rear of the vehicle to hit a wall. Seeing what was happening, the crew of another Panther further up the road fired and unintentionally hit the turret rear of the stricken Panther, starting a fire. Captain A.C. Vasser Hall heard the noise of the impact; the flames silhouetted the crew as they attempted to escape and were cut down by infantry fire. One crewman remained in the tank, but was shot as he appeared the next morning (Zuehlke 2005: 204). Vasser Hall was hit by stone fragments that momentarily floored him; he took shelter in a trench in the farm courtyard and had his wound dressed by the quartermaster, Captain Earl Rouatt.

Fuss wrote how they had withdrawn to regroup; Meyer then organized a double-pronged assault, with I. Zug (led by Fuss) moving to the north of the road while SS-Untersturmführer Fehling's II. Zug approached to the south of it (Meyer 2005a: 180). To support them, and with the direct route into the village blocked, Wünsche ordered 1./SS-PzRgt 12 south around Bretteville to attack from the west. The Panthers from the east were still firing incendiary rounds, which unintentionally resulted in the tanks swinging around the village to be silhouetted. SS-Sturmmann Leopold Lengheim, a Panther gunner in III. Zug, described the attack. The Panther of SS-Untersturmführer Paul Teichert, the II. Zug commander, was hit in the tracks and immobilized in the village. According to Lengheim, his Panther tried to reach Teichert, along with the tank of his platoon leader, SS-Untersturmführer Dietrich, but Allied personnel taking cover in a row of bushes some 100m away hit Dietrich's mount, prompting the crew to exit the tank. All but the radio operator succeeded and ran towards Lengheim's tank, which was firing at the bushes (Meyer 2005a: 181). Dietrich signalled to them to turn around and they retreated 500m to a firing position in a row of trees. Lengheim described how a virtual wall of fire hit his turret, wrecking the firing mechanism and killing his commander; the driver drove the tank into cover and was ordered to retreat to the repair shop.

The fight for Bretteville

German view: This scene shows soldiers from the platoon commanded by SS-Untersturmführer Reinhold Fuss as they attempt to get closer to the church. Some of the men are in the process of assaulting across the road from behind a building while under sporadic fire from Canadian infantry close by. They are attempting to reach an entrance to a courtyard. A variety of camouflage uniforms are worn by different members of Fuss's platoon. The other platoon involved in the attack was led by SS-Untersturmführer Fehling. Fuss later discovered that Fehling quickly withdrew after being detected by the Canadians; meanwhile, Fuss and only six men of his platoon had managed to get to the church. As planned, Fuss's party sent up a signal flare and waited for the German armour to arrive, but the Panzers never reached them (Meyer 2005a: 180).

Canadian view: This scene depicts the situation along the main road near the Canadian battalion headquarters during the German night attack on Bretteville-l'Orgueilleuse. The Panther that earlier tried to dash into the village is now burning. The PIAT team that hit the tank is now preparing for another attack. The Canadians have repulsed the initial attack, but German soldiers can be seen intermittently, trying to infiltrate into the village once their direct approach had failed. Armed with a Thompson submachine gun, Gunner William Milner of 13 Field Regiment RCA's headquarters defence section was standing in an alleyway when he glimpsed an MG 42 machine-gun team dash past him and climb over a stone wall at the end of the lane. He noticed his CO, Lieutenant-Colonel Freddie Clifford, chasing them and firing his revolver and was admonished by Clifford for not firing his own weapon.

SS-Untersturmführer Jürgen Chemnitz, the commander of I. Zug, 1./SS-PzRgt 12, described how he was also ordered to drive around the village to the south and enter from the west; he formed his tanks into a line to offer less of a target, but all three were hit, almost simultaneously. The engine compartment of the tank closest to Bretteville was burning, but the crew successfully baled out. The tank was destroyed later, perhaps by a PIAT. The platoon commander's turret was also hit, the loader was badly wounded and the electrical system failed. Chemnitz baled out and went over to the third tank, commanded by SS-Unterscharführer Rust, which had already survived many hits. Chemnitz radioed the company commander who told him to retreat. With his wounded loader, Chemnitz and two tanks withdrew. Fuss and six men had reached the church in Bretteville, but would not receive any armoured support.

While the work to repair his tank's electrical system was being carried out, Chemnitz dismounted and, armed with a submachine gun, decided to enter the village. He met the regimental orderly officer, SS-Untersturmführer Rudolf Nehrlich, armed with a Lee-Enfield rifle and rifle grenade; as the two men followed the garden walls along the street into the village, Chemnitz noticed the destroyed Panther in the village, still smouldering. Two trucks then rolled up; when the first was hit with a PIAT, German infantry were seen running to the rear and the second truck abruptly turned around. Chemnitz recalled how the pair sought cover behind a 2m-high wall, only to find themselves surrounded by Canadian troops. At 0400hrs the two German officers scrambled across a wall into a garden and then took cover in a willow tree. The Canadians seemed to be distracted and the officers both managed to leave the village and regain their own lines (Meyer 2005a: 180–81).

1 RRR had the support of 12 and 13 Field regiments RCA, 2km north of Bretteville with about ten Centaur self-propelled howitzers from 2 RMAS standing guard over the guns, but the artillery were exposed following the Canadian withdrawal from the River Mue. Clifford was with Matheson in his headquarters in a small *château* at the eastern end of Bretteville. 79 Medium Regiment RA was also ashore, but 6 and 191 Field regiments RA were delayed. A FOO was allocated to each infantry company. The guns had prepared targets the day before on likely enemy forming-up positions and approach routes. Sergeant J. Moffat of 13 Field Regiment RCA recalled being told to maintain his fire until all ammunition was expended (Milner 2014: 273). Here, an M7 Priest self-propelled gun is depicted on 6 June. (Ken Bell/ Canada. Dept. of National Defence / Library and Archives Canada / PA-131440)

On the other side of a low stone wall by battalion headquarters, Riflemen Gill Carnie, Clarence Hewitt and Joseph Lapointe with a PIAT occupied a trench and were out of sight of the lead Panther. Lapointe stood up and fired at the side armour from 14m, hitting but not destroying the tank. The Panther continued on for a few metres as the team reloaded. Regimental Sergeant Major Edwards had prepared some Type 75 anti-tank grenades to string across the road, but was unable to place the device; instead, the tank unintentionally set them off and the explosion broke the right track. Another PIAT round was fired and missed, but a third caused the rear of the vehicle to hit a wall. Here, the PIAT team inspect the Panther they destroyed. (Lieut. Donald I. Grant / Canada. Dept. of National Defence / Library and Archives Canada / PA-116529)

By 0230hrs on 9 June a stalemate was obvious to both sides. Matheson recalled that at times the Germans appeared to have detected a slackening-off of the Canadian effort (Milner 2014: 272). At 0315hrs a German armoured car 'ran up the main street and was knocked out by PIAT fire in front of our Bn HQ' (1 RRR War Diary: 3). A *Kübelwagen* also entered and an officer was hit by a PIAT round while dismounting to have a look around. Located near the regimental aid post (RAP) south-west of Bretteville, Company Sergeant Major Bill Currie fired his PIAT at two tanks that approached to within 50m. His loader, Irwin Wood, described how Currie fired as quickly as Wood could reload the PIAT, scoring several hits and disabling the nearer of the two tanks (Milner 2014: 270). They then watched as another Panther appeared and its crew dismounted, hooked up the disabled tank and drove away. Currie was seriously wounded bringing up more PIAT bombs, but Wood remained and observed a Panther destroyed by anti-tank fire near the road to Norrey.

The Panthers could not close within PIAT range without risking destruction and so stood off to target the buildings with gunfire. The 1 RRR War Diary reported that during the action 'we lost seven carriers one of which was loaded with ammunition. Five enemy panzers were knocked out in the vicinity of the command post', and also described how 'a hot time was had by all as enemy tanks were all about the town blasting away … destroying one of

Gordon Brown

Gordon Brown volunteered for service in 1941 and was commissioned into The Regina Rifle Regiment. In 1944 he was the 1 RRR transport officer and was given command of D Coy on 8 June. At Bretteville-l'Orgueilleuse, Matheson told his company commanders to ignore German tanks and worry about the infantry, but Brown remained wary of the enemy armour (Zuehlke 2005: 158). Out of infantry training for a year, Brown felt he lacked the martial qualities of Lieutenant Roberts, his 2IC, and Major Charles 'Stu' Tubb, OC C Coy (Zuehlke 2005: 202). At Cardonville Farm he decided on where to put his men and responded to enemy attacks by trying to redeploy heavy weapons to where they might be needed most. Sometimes this worked, but at other times it did not. He relied on his experienced officers and NCOs for guidance. He continued to command D Coy in Normandy and, except for two periods of absence because of wounds, until the end of the war. He was awarded the Distinguished Service Order in 1945 and in 1952 was promoted lieutenant-colonel and appointed commander of the battalion. He went on to serve on the staff before retiring to civilian life. He died in 2008.

our A/T guns. The whole sky was lit up by the blazing roofs and the burning tanks' (1 RRR War Diary: 3).

The German infantry were not having much success either. At 0530hrs, a priest discovered Fuss in the church. The Germans were on the balcony and had to run downstairs when Canadians entered. After loosing off automatic fire, Fuss's men sought to exit the church via a side door (Meyer 2005a: 183). Two of the Germans were shot before they could leave and the remainder took refuge in a hollow, where they would spend six days. They managed to dig a hole in the adjoining wall to break into the adjacent field. Two men asked to stay put; Fuss and two others crossed a field full of vehicles and reached woods near Norrey, where they joined up with the division. The two shot in the church – Zimmermann and Ziermann – were wounded and made prisoner.

At Cardonville Farm, Captain Brown noticed some Panthers that had decided to go around Norrey, but the two anti-tank guns in the orchard were covering open ground west towards Putot and could not see them. Sometime later he glanced out of the hole in the wall in the eastern courtyard, only to see a large tank moving close at hand; the Germans were using the rail crossing

Reinhold Fuss

In 1940 Reinhold Fuss was an *SS-Sturmmann* in 1. SS-Panzer-Division *Leibstandarte SS Adolf Hitler* and was commissioned in March 1943. He served on the Eastern Front before transferring to 12. SS-Panzer-Division *Hitlerjugend*. Serving as a platoon commander in 15./SS-PzGrenRgt 25 during the attack on Bretteville-l'Orgueilleuse, he quickly dismounted his men from the Panther tanks they were riding on while outside the village and attempted to rally them for an attack. His company commander was killed and he had to assume responsibility for the right wing. Leading from the front as most Waffen-SS officers did, Fuss managed to reach the church with six men, the rest being lost along the way. SS-Unterscharführer Flixeder, accompanying Fuss, was critical of his decision to go to the church. Despite this criticism, Fuss held his men together and would not let them surrender. Escaping from encirclement some days later, Fuss assumed command of the company and was promoted *SS-Obersturmführer*. He commanded the company in the remaining battles and survived the war.

nearby (Zuehlke 2005: 200). Panthers were seeking sanctuary in Cardonville Farm, but Brown was not unduly perturbed because they did not appear to be accompanied by infantry. He knew that armour could not successfully defend ground without supporting infantry, and could not understand why the Germans were acting in defiance of the usual tenets of armoured warfare. He went over to the FOO, whom he found asleep. Brown shook him awake and ordered him to contact headquarters, but the telephone line was already lost (Zuehlke 2005: 200–01). Brown then asked the gunners to move their anti-tank guns to the other side of the orchard to fire on the Panthers. The sergeant in command of the anti-tank guns was against the idea as they might draw enemy fire, but Brown told him the company HQ would be overrun otherwise and he agreed to move.

Meanwhile, according to Brown, Company Sergeant Major Jimmy Jacobs was organizing D Coy (Zuehlke 2005: 201). At the command post the signaller was trying to raise battalion headquarters, but there was nothing but noise on the radio. Then Tubb's voice was heard and Brown, with a hint of desperation, asked him what he should do about the tanks roaming all over his area. The anti-tank guns had not moved, the sergeant informed him, because tanks had surrounded the orchard. Able to hear the tanks' engines, Brown spread the word to hold fire as he hoped to organize a coordinated attack on the tanks by several of his men armed with 'sticky' bombs. Then Corporal Ritchie fired his Sten submachine gun as two German tank commanders dismounted. German turrets slowly swung around towards the farm buildings and their guns began to fire tracer bullets indiscriminately. The barn was full of dry hay and was soon ablaze. The Canadians grabbed as much ammunition as they could and vacated the barn; in the orchard the two anti-tank guns were destroyed, and the Panthers were running amok (Zuehlke 2005: 204). At 0445hrs the FOO radioed that he was surrounded by tanks; he was found dead in his carrier the next day.

A high thick wooden gate barred entrance to the compound and a string of Type 75 anti-tank grenades were quickly hung behind the barrier

At 1300hrs on 9 June, Panthers of 3./SS-PzRgt 12 (visible here in Rots earlier in the day with troops from 15./SS-PzGrenRgt 25) were ordered to race south of the railway embankment towards Norrey from la Villeneuve. At first, 12 Panthers were protected, but their side armour was exposed to gunfire from recently arrived Shermans, some equipped with 17-pdr guns, once the cutting and level crossing were reached. Seven Panthers were knocked out. 13 Field Regiment RCA also supported the Shermans and hampered the progress of the German infantry. Entrenched south of Norrey, I./SS-PzGrenRgt 26 was supposed to join in the attack. (ullstein bild/ullstein bild via Getty Images)

to prevent access. A German tank lumbered up and knocked the gate down, but was discouraged from pushing on and rumbled around the farm's east wall, firing shells into the building. Unsure whether his battalion had survived the armoured attack, Brown thought an infantry assault would soon follow (Zuehlke 2005: 207). Mohnke, the commander of SS-Panzergrenadier-Regiment 26, was focused on his western flank at Putot, however, and distracted with enforcing his order not to accept prisoners. He was furious that earlier in the day SS-Sturmbannführer Bernhard Siebken, the commander of II./SS-PzGrenRgt 26, had dispatched 40 prisoners to the rear. In the evening Mohnke intercepted them and soon after they were executed. As a result Meyer was unable to support the tanks with the infantry they needed and at 0430hrs, with dawn approaching, decided to retreat to Rots. Wünsche was injured in the knee by artillery shrapnel while dismounting from his Panther. 1./SS-PzGrenRgt 26 occupied Rots, and some Panthers took up ambush positions there; 2. and 3./SS-PzGrenRgt 26 were south of Norrey.

Having moved around Norrey, at 0600hrs 2./SS-PzGrenRgt 26 belatedly launched an infantry assault on Cardonville Farm. Expecting little resistance, the company made a direct approach across the railway line unsupported by artillery or tanks, and many German infantry were cut down. Another attempt was organized and Lieutenant R. Roberts, company 2IC D Coy, took a section to the upper storey of the farm where he could target a railway cutting being used to form up the German assault troops. Brown could see German infantry crawling through the wheat; attempts to reach Matheson on the radio brought only German voices asking if they were lonely. As Brown took some 1 CHO soldiers and their medium machine gun to the upper storey, tracer rounds hit one of the crew, detonating two grenades the Cameron Highlander was carrying (Zuehlke 2005: 208).

German artillery and mortar fire began to land on the farm and with the roof blasted open, the defenders observed the farm that the Germans were using as a base south of the railway line. Jacobs believed grenades would soon be thrown over the wall and warning calls told the men when to take cover. Eventually, Matheson was reached on the radio; he asked Clifford to organize a bombardment. Brown told him the coordinates and reported that his men could last only another 20 minutes; he was told to take cover as the bombardment would be close to their positions. Soon after, a deafening 10-minute bombardment hit the German-held farm, while the Canadian positions were untouched (Zuehlke 2005: 210). The German attack was blunted. D Coy had suffered 50 per cent casualties. Only two men survived in the orchards.

During the attack on Bretteville, SS-Panzergrenadier-Regiment 25 suffered one officer, five NCOs and 13 men killed; one officer, one NCO and 14 men wounded; and one officer, one NCO and seven men missing. SS-Panzer-Regiment 12 lost two officers, three NCOs and seven men killed; four officers, three NCOs and 23 men wounded; and no missing. I./SS-PzGrenRgt 26 lost two NCOs and ten men killed; six NCOs and 42 men wounded; and one man missing. Three Panthers were written off and two badly damaged. In the *Official History of the Canadian Army in the Second World War*, Colonel C.P. Stacey described how the German operations gave the impression of rather hasty and ineffective improvisation. The attacks displayed courage and determination, but no particular tactical skill.

Hill 168

15 August 1944

BACKGROUND TO BATTLE

In late July 1944 Operation *Goodwood*, designed to break out from the ever-growing Allied bridgehead, failed to meet expectations. A mainly armoured thrust supported by heavy aerial bombing was blunted and attention turned to the US offensive in the west. Here, the German defences relied less on Waffen-SS Panzer divisions and were more brittle as a result. A breakthrough

On the night of 7/8 August, Operation *Totalize* began; armoured columns comprising tanks and infantry from 8th and 9th Canadian Infantry brigades mounted in Kangaroo APCs (modified M7 Priest self-propelled artillery guns) advanced into positions that had suffered an aerial bombardment by strategic bombers. Here, these APCs, along with tanks, are depicted prior to the start of the offensive. (Barnet / Canada. Dept. of National Defence / Library and Archives Canada / PA-129172)

Operation *Tractable* was another Allied offensive that employed mass armour. Tanks were organized into tight formations with the intention of overrunning the enemy using overwhelming force. 3rd Canadian Infantry Division with 2nd Canadian Armoured Brigade attacked the eastern flank; 4th Canadian Armoured Division attacked the western flank. Here, the formations prepare prior to the start of the offensive. (Lieut. Donald I. Grant / Canada. Dept. of National Defence / Library and Archives Canada / PA-113659)

was achieved and Lieutenant General George Patton's Third US Army fanned out to exploit into the interior. One arm of this armoured pincer turned south-east and then north-east in order to envelop the German front. At the same time First Canadian Army and Second British Army were both tasked with a southerly advance to break the German line and meet up with the Americans. Some 350,000 German soldiers were in the rapidly developing 'Falaise Pocket'. Hitler insisted on an offensive at Mortain with the intention of cutting off the US spearheads from their supply bases, but results were disappointing and the German attack only served to delay escape from the pocket.

Montgomery gave the task of capturing Falaise to First Canadian Army. On the night of 7/8 August, Operation *Totalize* began. Initial results were promising, but while Hill 195 north-east of Falaise was captured, strong German armoured counter-attacks limited the extent of the success and mauled elements of 4th Canadian Armoured Division. The commander of 3rd Canadian Infantry Division, Major-General Rod Keller, was removed from command. The offensive ended on 13 August, as no breakthrough had been achieved, but the following day the Canadians with 1st Polish Armoured Division in support launched Operation *Tractable*. The Allies knew the recently arrived 85. Infanterie-Division was on both sides of the River Laison with 89. and 272. Infanterie-Divisionen either side, but the positions of the Waffen-SS formations were undefined. Little resistance was expected and Montgomery thought Falaise would be captured by midnight.

Having suffered 6,164 casualties to 20 July and been provided with hardly any replacements, *Hitlerjugend* had had little respite since the Normandy invasion. The *Goodwood* offensive caused further losses and infantry battalions were each down to two weak companies. Kurt Meyer was in command following the death of Witt when l'Abbaye d'Ardenne was targeted by a naval bombardment. Meyer was also responsible for

By the evening of 13 August, the 13 Tiger tanks of schwere SS-Panzer-Abteilung 102 were deployed throughout the area north of Falaise. SS-Unterscharführer Streng, a Tiger commander, wrote that when Operation *Tractable* began, the order to pull back to the north-east of Falaise was received. They were targeted by Allied fighter-bombers in the pale light of the early morning, but used the cover of some woods to good effect and lost no vehicles. They approached the River Laison and lost three tanks to Shermans. The rest of the Tigers hit 19 tanks from 1st Hussars as they attempted to cross the river. (Galerie Bilderwelt/Getty Images)

two infantry divisions. Along with Wünsche, he scouted north of Falaise for suitable positions and found high ground 4km north of the city that, while open and exposed to Allied artillery fire, was good terrain in which to dig in. The division's role in preventing an Allied breakthrough during Operation *Totalize* was something Meyer attempted to repeat during Operation *Tractable*. The lack of German troop strength precluded a solid defensive line and the front line comprised interlocking firing positions. On the right, SS-Panzer-Regiment 12 defended Hill 159. Further west, I. and III./SS-PzGrenRgt 26 were given Soulagny and Hill 168, north-west of Falaise; they formed a battlegroup under SS-Sturmbannführer Bernhard Krause, with two Tiger tanks of schwere SS-Panzer-Abteilung 102 in support. III./SS-PzGrenRgt 26 was positioned to the right of I./SS-PzGrenRgt 26, but without its few remaining APCs, which were used as prime movers for artillery pieces. Some PzKpfw IV tanks from II./SS-PzRgt 12 were available. South-east of Falaise, III./SS-PzArtRgt 12 could fire in support and had plentiful ammunition as a stack of 10.5cm shells had been discovered in a rail siding in the town.

Meyer had a copy of the orders for the Allied offensive as a staff officer from a reconnaissance regiment with instructions that outlined the plan had strayed into German lines in his scout car on the night of 13/14 August and was intercepted. As a result, Lieutenant-General Guy Simonds, GOC II Canadian Corps, thought Meyer had positioned his forces along the expected line of advance. Hubert Meyer thought no movements could be made in time. The Germans immediately before the offensive did manage to conduct an artillery bombardment that caused few casualties, but did destroy some combat-support vehicles. In the event, 300 Allied tanks and four brigades of infantry descended on 41 German tanks and two infantry regiments, many of whose personnel had not seen action before.

MAP KEY

1 Early morning, 15 August: Under command of 2nd Canadian Armoured Brigade, 1 CSR occupies Hill 175.

2 1230hrs, 15 August: 1 CSR and tanks of 1st Hussars begin their advance towards Hill 168, defended by III./SS-PzGrenRgt 26 and some supporting tanks. Two Canadian companies lead, with another two following behind.

3 1300hrs, 15 August: D Coy advances to the first hedge and calls for armoured support after spotting German tanks behind the second hedge. Two Shermans are destroyed. Members of a PIAT team are killed when sent against a German tank, perhaps a Tiger – though this tank, with another, withdraws 400m.

4 1320hrs, 15 August: Although disabled, another Sherman hits a German tank and causes it to go up in flames.

5 1330hrs, 15 August: B Coy clears the long hedge and advances towards a barn on a ridge to the west. A German tank fires at the company headquarters, but moves away when targeted by a PIAT.

6 1500hrs, 15 August: The carrier of the battalion commander, Lieutenant-Colonel Lendrum, is hit. He is slightly wounded and the battalion signals radio is destroyed.

7 c.1500hrs, 15 August: A Coy, following behind D Coy, passes the second hedge and is targeted by three German tanks. Company Sergeant Major John Grimmond drives them away with a PIAT and establishes an alternative command post.

8 Mid-afternoon, 15 August: 1 CSR occupies Hill 168. A Canadian artillery bombardment mistakenly targets battalion positions.

9 1815hrs, 15 August: 1 RWR advances on Soulagny, defended by I./SS-PzGrenRgt 26. Two Tigers of 2./sSS-PzAbt 102 intervene to throw the Canadians out of the village. 1 RWR retires.

10 Evening, 15 August: B Sqn, Fort Garry Horse is attacked by Tigers and all further attacks by 7th Canadian Infantry Brigade are suspended.

Battlefield environment

The terrain in front of Hill 168 'was a succession of flat wheatfields with thick hedges which meant advancing without cover through intense fire' (Henderson). A chequer-board of small fields bordered by tall hedgerows allowed the Germans to open fire from concealed positions. The hedgerows were used to cover the defenders' withdrawal to the next field. The terrain was also described as a 'maze of almost insurmountable hedgerows, behind which lurked machine guns and TIGER tanks' (Citations).

9th Canadian Infantry Brigade was soon mopping up German forces in the Laison Valley, but Allied armour had trouble finding suitable crossing places over the river. Lieutenant-General Simonds, GOC II Canadian Corps, wanted to drive on to Falaise during the night, but the disorganization created by the strategic bombers, the loss of 4th Canadian Armoured Brigade's commander, and fording the river all required action. (Lieut. H. Gordon Aikman / Canada. Dept. of National Defence / Library and Archives Canada / PA-162450)

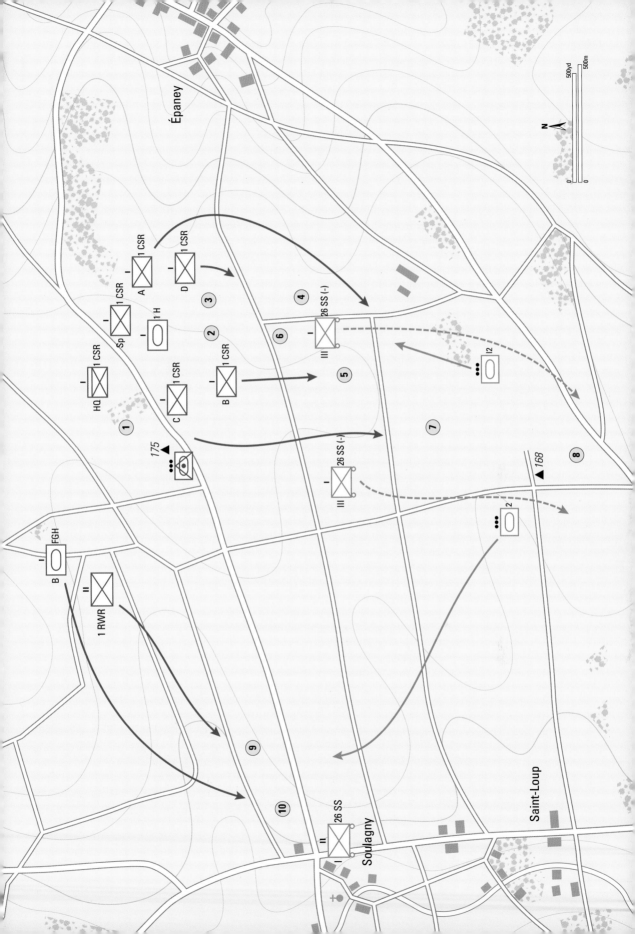

INTO COMBAT

To assist command and control, Operation *Tractable* started at 1200hrs on 14 August in daylight. The attack got off to a faltering start as strategic bombers had difficulty determining their targets and caused 500 Allied casualties as well as damage to German positions. With 9th Canadian Infantry Brigade still mopping up in the Laison Valley, 7th Canadian Infantry Brigade (including 1 CSR without APCs) was ordered to take over the following day and move on high ground north-west of Falaise. 4th Canadian Armoured Division with support from 1st Polish Armoured Division would attack Hill 159. 2nd Canadian Infantry Division was available as a reserve.

Commanded by Major R. Lendrum, as Lieutenant-Colonel Fred Cabeldu was ill, 1 CSR (37 officers and 811 other ranks) travelled 6.4km and, having seen no enemy, crossed the River Laison south of Rouvres at 1930hrs on 14 August. At 0100hrs on 15 August they reached Hill 175 with hardly any casualties and dug in. Lendrum's battalion, under the command of 2nd Canadian Armoured Brigade, was out in front, with other battalions of 7th Canadian Infantry Brigade – 1 RWR and 1 RRR – behind.

Lendrum described how at 1000hrs on 15 August he 'was called away to HQ 2nd Cdn Armd Bde, where he found the Bn was under the command the Armd Bde and was to attack Point 168 about 1½ Kms to the Sth' (Lendrum). Lieutenant-Colonel Ray Colwell was the temporary commander of the brigade and told him to advance 1 mile (1.6km) to Objective Idaho, the name given to Hill 168, at 1130hrs. The area offered superb views of the road to Falaise; Colwell told Lendrum little resistance should be expected. Allied artillery had not kept up with the advance during Operation *Totalize* and the artillery commander requested postponement of the attack by a day, but this was refused. A squadron of 1st Hussars (11 Shermans) commanded by Major Brandon Conron and a platoon of M10 self-propelled guns were in support. Lieutenant-Colonel John Meldram's 1 RWR would follow on and attack Soulagny.

At 1300hrs the battalion was at last ready and advanced in box formation with D Coy and B Coy leading, followed by A Coy and C Coy. Lendrum's headquarters was in the centre. B Coy was not commanded by Major P. Ramsey; instead, Captain David Pugh was in charge, supported by Lieutenant Park who commanded the advance guard. Mortar, machine-gun and sniper fire immediately targeted the Canadian company as they advanced to the first hedge and the men took cover. Ramsey later reported that Pugh had '2 pls up (11 Pl right and 12 Pl left)' (Ramsey); snipers and two machine guns were firing from the first hedge and this was cleared with support from the M10s. A long hedge ran perpendicular and split 12 Platoon as they advanced, but another two machine guns were cleared from the hedge. Then 11 Platoon and the balance of 12 Platoon were sent to a ridge to the right and were fired upon by two tanks. They moved into an area called 'the rectangle' to the right of the ridge and cleared a barn. Lieutenant Lorimer from 12 Platoon was wounded. A tank behind a hedge fired at company headquarters, but moved away when targeted by a PIAT.

A Coy, 1 CSR, commanded by Major W. Mathews, 'quickly moved up and took up posns to the left of 'D' Coy … and ran into considerable difficulty when we flushed 6 ENEMY TANKS. Sgt Clarke, commanding 7 Pl, and Cpl Dodd of the same Pl did a grand job here stalking the TANKS with PIATS so successfully that they took flight' (Mathews). Here, a Tiger appears in Normandy. (Bundesarchiv Bild 101I-299-1805-21 Foto: Scheck)

never did make an appearance'; instead, once Hill 168 was reached, two men attempted to get their PIAT in place when a German tank (probably a Tiger) appeared, but missed their target. 'Fortunately the tank's main object was apparently escape, for it passed us by without firing a shot' (Gallagher).

B Coy also had a close experience of tanks. Captain Pugh, Company Sergeant Major John Grimmond and a signaller were taking cover in a ditch from shells and were unsuccessfully trying to call for tank support on the radio amid the din. When some tanks approached they were thought to be friendly, but turned out to be German; many Canadian soldiers survived the experience only because of the good cover. One soldier called to a tank commander in his turret who turned out to be German. 1 CSR's mortar platoon had to dismount from their carriers and fight their way forward with light machine guns and rifles. When they were momentarily stopped by tanks, 'the mortar section in support fired from open positions on the enemy … [when targeted] they would withdraw slightly, set up their mortar, and blast away again' (Mortar).

Lendrum reported his battalion was 'advancing from hedge to hedge with some support from tanks against brisk fire from MGs, mortars, and tanks' (Lendrum); at 1500hrs his carrier was destroyed. He was not in the carrier at the time, but the radio was destroyed and the companies were out of touch with each other. Communication with brigade and the companies went instead via the set in the battalion half-track, which 'was slow, but worked moderately well' (Lendrum). There was still difficulty in effecting liaison and Company Sergeant Major Grimmond from B Coy was ordered to establish the company signals section in cover. He found three tanks in the area and 'routed the enemy tanks with a PIAT and established his Coy HQ and the wireless links; by moving from place to place, and simulating a stronger force, this WO was able to maintain the coy position, and thereby maintain the success of the Operation' (Citations). Only by 1700hrs would the communications situation improve for the Canadians.

At 1530hrs, artillery was available to the Canadians, but it laid down fire on battalion positions before moving on to German positions. Gallagher described 'the most terrifying shelling any of us have experienced' (Gallagher). The platoon did not suffer any casualties as a result of the artillery bombardment, but was badly shaken up. The men then dug into the rocky soil on Hill 168. During the attack, 33 other ranks were killed and 119 wounded, mostly from the forward companies. Seven officers were wounded. The 1st Hussars War Diary reported only two Shermans destroyed. Ramsey reported that his men showed 'great disregard to the enemy fire and many showed coolness and courage well above the average, especially under the TANK guns which they could see' (Ramsey). In D Coy, as there were many new men that were taking part in their first attack, there was a tendency to go to ground and the officers and NCOs 'urged them on until the advance went steadily forward at great speed' (Henderson). Henderson was awarded a Distinguished Service Order for his 'courage and leadership under heavy fire' (Citations).

Colwell then ordered 1 RWR to assault Soulagny on the Falaise road. A Coy gained the village, but was assaulted by two Tigers and infantry and lost half its strength before withdrawing. A Tiger commander who was screening the road between Soulagny and Saint-Pierre reported how that evening a Waffen-SS company commander asked the Tiger platoon commander to rescue his men; the tank commander, a former infantryman, agreed to help. The Tigers drove quickly across country to Soulagny where a line of half a dozen Shermans

The 1 CSR regimental aid post (RAP) was by the battalion headquarters and jeeps had difficulty bringing in casualties. The carriers were brought up and were very useful as they gave protection against mortar and shell fire. During the assault, 125 casualties would pass through the RAP, though not without problems. The company sergeant major of C Coy reported how 'The snipers in the long hedge were not cleared out and they continued to shoot at our walking wounded returning to our R.A.P.' (CSM). Here, Canadian wounded are being evacuated in Normandy. (Canada. Dept. of National Defence / Library and Archives Canada / PA-130176)

and would not be available until the Falaise battles; by then the Allies had an overall superiority in men and *matériel* to limit the difference the German infantry divisions could make.

The situation immediately following the Normandy landings was entirely different. On 7 June, 9th Canadian Infantry Brigade was vulnerable because British brigades could not guarantee the flanks. Tasked with capturing Carpiquet, at Buron and Authie 1 NNSH, assisted by 50 tanks from The Sherbrooke Fusiliers Regiment, initially defeated a battlegroup from 21. Panzer-Division equipped with artillery and anti-tank guns. Then they encountered a Waffen-SS infantry battalion and elements of another with artillery and armoured support. The Canadians' training made them tenacious opponents in defence, but lack of artillery severely hampered them. The German attackers might have suffered severe losses in the open fields outside Authie, but German radio interference, lack of observers and orders that some artillery should move forward meant no Canadian artillery was called in. Once the strength of German defences was appreciated, 1 NNSH should have stayed at les Buissons. Carpiquet was untenable as long as Saint-Contest remained in German hands and, as Milner has shown, the

At Authie on 8 July 1944 the Germans sent 5./SS-PzRgt 12 (equipped with PzKpfw IV tanks) to assist the defenders once the attack started. Panthers of I. and II. Züge, 3./SS-PzRgt 12 also carried out an attack. Seven Panthers and five PzKpfw IV tanks were lost. Here, a destroyed Panther is examined near Authie in July. (Gordon Aikman / Canada. Dept. of National Defence / Library and Archives Canada / PA-114367)

Canadian soldiers gain some protection outside a village in Normandy. (Lieut. Ken Bell / Canada. Dept. of National Defence / Library and Archives Canada / PA-129043)

intermediate objective that the Canadian battalion was endeavouring to capture – the high ground between Authie and Buron – did not exist. Despite a lack of combined-arms training and a compromising situation, coordination between the Canadian infantry and armour unit commanders saved 1 NNSH from annihilation.

The Germans then decided to move against 7th Canadian Infantry Brigade on the Bayeux road, but ran into well-prepared defences in strong defensive terrain. At Bretteville-l'Orgueilleuse and Putot the Canadians fought according to the operational plan to halt the Panzer attack. The terrain was relatively open both here and north of Caen and tanks could threaten the Allied lodgement. Rommel had wanted three divisions on that ground, but Hitler would not agree to it. The commitment of elements of 21. Panzer-Division north of Caen to stall capture of the city made them unable to support an attack along the River Mue. The advance on Carpiquet prevented SS-Panzergrenadier-Regiment 25 participating.

SS-Panzergrenadier-Regiment 26 was deployed thin on the ground further west. The German attack on Bretteville during the night and early morning of 8/9 June thus lacked infantry and showed up the inefficiencies of Waffen-SS senior commanders. Mohnke failed to support the attack until the following morning when tank support was not available. His infantry had travelled to the front on 7 June and had been involved in combat against Norrey since early morning on 8 June; once ready to commence an attack on 9 June they were disrupted by timely Canadian use of artillery and resolute infantry in good cover. German devolution of command and control had hampered the organization of the Bretteville attack. Elements of the Panzer-Lehr-Division could have supported the Waffen-SS, but Generalleutnant Fritz Bayerlein, the division's commander, suggested he would advance only if *Hitlerjugend* had already cleared the way. Instead, he had started moving the Panzer-Lehr-Division further west once he realized the Canadians were in Norrey in strength.

The Canadian defence of the villages around the River Mue was decisive in stemming the German Panzer counter-attack. The failure of the counter-attack put the Germans on the defensive and the Allies began to wear down their line in order to obtain a breakthrough. This was a slow process as the Canadians found they lacked the necessary assault artillery and heavily armoured tanks necessary to capture fortified villages quickly. Aerial assault and artillery bombardments to destroy these positions were not effective. The development of Kangaroo APCs helped bring the Canadian infantry closer to their targets, but they had to do the hard work and dismount to capture objectives. The ability of field artillery to neutralize German weapons once battle commenced depended on forward observers witnessing the fall of shot and calling fire down accurately. German positions prior to the start of an offensive were usually well camouflaged and not always detected by aerial photo reconnaissance. Instead, heavy artillery and naval guns were better at battlefield interdiction to prevent German reinforcements being brought up.

By the start of Operation *Tractable* the German divisions, lacking reinforcements, were vulnerable to Allied formations that time and again were brought up to full strength, but the Canadians had to break through the last defensive position in front of Falaise that was manned by recently arrived infantry divisions. On Hill 168 the Canadians would again have to fight initially without artillery support – and when the guns were able to fire, their own troops were targeted. Infantry supported by some tanks had to advance against Waffen-SS positions in cover that were supported by Tiger and PzKpfw IV tanks. Undeterred, the Canadians were resolute and with PIATs held their ground and advanced towards the hill. Canadian tank support was also effective. The Germans inflicted a heavy price in casualties, however, and 1 CSR was forced to sit tight and was unavailable for offensive operations for two days. Rather than holding the infantry responsible for the slow progress in closing the ground to US forces at Argentan, Simmonds sacked Major-General George Kitching, GOC 4th Canadian Armoured Division. The Falaise gap would be finally closed on 21 August. About 50,000 Germans were taken prisoner, but the haul was smaller than the Allies expected.

Aftermath

Following the defensive battles in early June 1944, 3rd Canadian Infantry Division spent the rest of the month rebuilding. The formation would have the highest casualty rate of any Allied division in Normandy. Buron was captured at last on 8 July during Operation *Charnwood* – not by 1 NNSH, but by 1st Battalion, Highland Light Infantry of Canada (1 HLIC), also part of 9th Canadian Infantry Brigade, supported by a Sherbrooke Fusiliers squadron of Shermans and specialist Churchill tanks as well as a battery of M10 self-propelled guns. A rolling barrage was declined by the Canadian battalion commander for fear of hitting his own troops. Few of the German weapons were destroyed by field artillery. The Canadian infantry had to do the work of clearing out German positions initially without armour support (some tanks had run into a minefield and their crews were reluctant to move forward, though others did eventually target German positions with direct fire). The Waffen-SS tanks were dealt with by the M10s, but seven of the self-propelled guns were lost, along with 11 Shermans. 1 HLIC suffered 262 casualties. That same day in Villons-les-Buissons, 1 NNSH advanced on Authie once Buron was captured. 1 RRR was tasked with advancing on l'Abbaye d'Ardenne following the capture of Buron. A rolling barrage was accepted by the battalion and a squadron of tanks advanced in support. The abbey fell to 1 RRR that night, but 216 casualties were sustained. German resistance was broken and Caen fell on 9 July. By the end of July 1 RRR had suffered 678 casualties, including 185 killed.

The pursuit following the Normandy break-out was a high point for the Canadians. Once Falaise was captured, 3rd Canadian Infantry Division felt an immense sense of achievement that would sustain morale until the gruelling battles for the Scheldt Estuary in October and November 1944 and those for the northern wooded German plain early in 1945. The emphasis was again on the infantry, fighting in difficult terrain. They wanted tanks to

While *Hitlerjugend* continued to fight in the front line, with the advance of the Allied armies into Germany Hitler Youth were recruited into the Volkssturm (People's Army) that also took recruits up to the age of 60. In late March 1945 Axmann formed special tank-hunting squads from 2,000 Hitler Youth recruits. (Heinrich Hoffmann/ullstein bild via Getty Images)

assume the lead role, but crews were reluctant and wished to assist the infantry from positions to the rear. The Canadians relied upon artillery barrages to suppress rather than destroy German defences in order to cover the infantry's movements. Canadian infantry had to close with the Germans and use fire-and-movement tactics to outflank the enemy. Replacements were brought in – not many original recruits remained – but Canadian combat effectiveness was not significantly lowered.

Following the capture of Hill 168, Krause's battlegroup defended Falaise with 150 infantry, two Tiger tanks and two 7.5cm anti-tank guns, and were attacked by 2nd Canadian Infantry Division. The last remnants of Krause's battlegroup were holed up in the school that was eventually captured on the night of 17/18 August. Despite heavy losses, according to Hubert Meyer, *Hitlerjugend* escaped from encirclement with 12,500 men remaining (this included 2,500 supply personnel). Losses to the infantry were of course disproportionately severe compared with the rest of the divisional units. Mohnke was transferred to 1. SS-Panzer-Division *Leibstandarte SS Adolf Hitler* and Krause assumed command of SS-Panzergrenadier-Regiment 26. Mohnke would end up commanding a battlegroup in Berlin in 1945. He survived the war and was held by the Soviets before his release in 1955. He died in 2001. Kurt Meyer was captured in September 1944 and Hubert Meyer was temporarily the division's commander. The division was re-formed with the influx of mainly unwilling recruits from the Luftwaffe and Kriegsmarine. Rapid promotions and an influx of officers brought in from other formations were not sufficient to provide enough junior leaders. During the Ardennes offensive in December 1944 another 9,870 men were lost. The division then moved to Hungary and participated in the Balaton Offensive in March 1945. Retreat followed and in May the *Hitlerjugend* survivors surrendered to US forces.

UNIT ORGANIZATIONS

Canadian

By 1944 the infantry battalion (801 men) was based on four rifle companies plus a support company fielding mortar, carrier, anti-tank and pioneer platoons; heavy machine guns were grouped into their own battalions and assigned to battalions by the divisional commander as and when required. A rifle company (127 men) had three platoons, each with three ten-man sections. Company Headquarters had two 2in mortars and three PIAT teams. There was also a small battalion headquarters staff and an HQ Company with a signals and an administration platoon. Battalion transport assigned a truck to every platoon to transport equipment.

German

A Waffen-SS *Panzergrenadier-Bataillon* comprised three *Panzergrenadier-Kompanien* and a *schwere* (heavy) *Kompanie*. The *Panzergrenadier-Kompanie* had three *Panzergrenadier-Züge*, a *schwere Zug* (fielding a *Granatwerfer-Gruppe* with two 8cm mortars and two *Maschinengewehr-Gruppen* each with two MG 42 medium machine guns), and a *Panzerjäger-Gruppe* with two 8.8cm *Panzerschreck* rocket launchers. The *Panzergrenadier-Zug* had three *Gruppen*, each comprising 12 men: two MG 42 teams (gunner and loader), a section leader with an MP 40 submachine gun, an assistant leader with an automatic rifle, five riflemen and a driver. The *schwere Kompanie* had a *Granatwerfer-Zug* (six 8cm mortars), an *Infanterie-Geschütz-Zug* (four 7.5cm infantry guns) and a *Panzerjäger-Zug* (three 7.5cm anti-tank guns).

BIBLIOGRAPHY

Primary sources

War Diary, 1 NNSH at http://lmharchive.ca/wp-content/uploads/2014/02/The-North-Nova-Scotia-Highlanders.pdf

War Diary, 1 RRR at http://lmharchive.ca/wp-content/uploads/2014/03/The-Regina-Rifle-Regiment.pdf

War Diary, 1 CSR at http://lmharchive.ca/wp-content/uploads/2014/03/The-Canadian-Scottish-Regiment.pdf

Canadian Scottish Regiment (Princess Mary's) Regimental Records Series XI Box 4.21 held by University of Victoria comprising: 'A' Company Report on attack on Hill 168 by Major W. Mathews; 'B' Company Report on attack on Hill 168 by Lieutenant J. Gallagher; 'B' Company by Major P. Ramsey; Notes on the Scottish by Major R. Lendrum; The Attack on Hill 168 by Major E. Henderson; Citations; The R.A.P. by C.S.M; The Mortar Platoon Attack on Hill 168.

Secondary sources

Butler, Rupert (2003). *SS-Hitlerjugend: The History of the Twelfth SS Division 1943–45*. London: Amber Books.

Hart, Russell A. (2001). *Clash of Arms: How the Allies Won in Normandy*. Boulder, CO: Lynne Rienner.

Jentz, T.L. (1996). *Panzer Truppen 2. The Complete Guide to the Creation and Employment of Germany's Tank Force*. Atglen, PA: Schiffer Publishing.

Luther, Craig (1987). *Blood and Honour: The History of the 12th SS Panzer Division, Hitler Youth, 1943–45*. San Jose, CA: R. James Bender.

Meyer, Hubert (2005a). *The 12th SS: The History of the Hitler Youth Panzer Division, Volume 1*. Mechanicsburg, PA: Stackpole.

Meyer, Hubert (2005b). *The 12th SS: The History of the Hitler Youth Panzer Division, Volume 2*. Mechanicsburg, PA: Stackpole.

Milner, Marc (2014). *Stopping the Panzers: The Untold Story of D Day*. Lawrence, KS: University Press of Kansas.

Peterson, Michael (2009). *Baby Division*. Morrisville, NC: Lulu.

Veldhoen, W. (2014). *The Canadian Scottish: A regiment like any other?* Utrecht: University of Utrecht.

Zuehlke, Mark (2005). *Holding Juno: Canada's Heroic Defence of the D-Day Beaches, June 7–12 1944*. Vancouver: Douglas & MacIntyre.

INDEX

References to illustrations are shown in **bold**.